A MESSAGE FROM THE SPHINX

ENEL

" There are more things in heaven and earth, Horatio,
Than are dreamt of in our philosophy. . . ."

SHAKESPEARE.

With 34 Illustrations

LONDON: RIDER & CO.
PATERNOSTER HOUSE, E.C.

Made and Printed in Great Britain at
The Mayflower Press, Plymouth.   William Brendon & Son, Ltd.
1936

Kessinger Publishing's Rare Reprints
Thousands of Scarce and Hard-to-Find Books!

We kindly invite you to view our extensive catalog list at:
http://www.kessinger.net

Some books by the same author :

1. *Trilogie de la Rota.*   A study of Hebraic Cabala.

2. *La Langue Sacrée.*   A study of the symbolism of hieroglyphic writing.

3. *Les Origines de la Genèse et l'Enseignement des Temples de l'Ancienne Egypte.*   Vol. I—A comparative study of the book of Genesis and of Egyptian texts concerning Creation.

CONTENTS

LIST OF ILLUSTRATIONS

LIST OF TABLES AND PLATES

PREFACE

THE MESSAGE

"I AM Tem, the Only One, the Reason of life, the Unique Source of every existence.

"I am the One who was before Time was. Before the Sun rose for the first time to light the world—I existed.

"Ra is my word, emanated from me to illuminate the world and to enlighten the reason of man.

"I said my first word and the Light came to life in the form of the Sun that rose over the horizon. Its rays bring life and light as they emanate from my word.

"I am the mother that conceived all life. I am the father that generated all living beings.

"I have no father or mother, as I am myself the Unique generator, the Sole principle of every life. I alone am the father and the mother of all beings, the Unique Source of every form of existence.

"I am the one of millions of years, the Only One who existed for ever and whose life is Eternity.

"My image is in every manifestation of life. I created man to my image.

"One generation passeth on to another among men, and I who know character have hidden myself.

"I am one who confoundeth by what is seen of the eyes.

"Let me be served in my fashion whether made

of precious stones, or fashioned of copper, like water replaced by water.

"There is no stream that suffereth itself to be hidden, it bursteth the dyke by which it was hidden. So do I not suffer to be captured in a visible form.

"My reflection is in this stone image since the world has come to exist fashioned by those who lived to glorify me on earth, and I will live in this image of mine till the end.

"But let not man confound me with this image of mine, as it is not I—and I not it. It is the visible reflection of my glory erected to teach men to serve me and adore me in this fashion.

"When man forgot that he was only one among thousands of my creations, I destroyed him and allowed my image to disappear—it was covered by the sand of the desert for thousands of years, but then came men to whose reason I unveiled the great mystery of my being, they understood and adored me, and I allowed them to uncover my image and to worship it.

"This happened thousands of years ago, my image is unveiled since and other men adore me under other names. I live in their hearts and in their temples under other forms, but this eternal image of mine is not adored, as they do not know that I am the Same, the Unchangeable, the Only One.

"This image of mine is venerated by the men who adore me under other names. They venerate it for they know that it is an image of God of ancient times. But they don't conceive that I am the Same, the Only One, who exists for ever.

"This image of mine is as old as the earth, and its life is the life of the earth.

" The sand of the desert, the hand of man—
nothing could destroy this image of mine. It is
worn by time, as is the earth, it approaches its end,
as the earth approaches its death, but I am eternal
and will never die.

" So will not die the man who believes in me and
worships me—he will live for ever in me, as he is my
living image. . . ."

From *Different Egyptian Papyri.*

Who hath ears to hear, let him hear. . . .

INTRODUCTORY

GENERAL OUTLINE OF THE WHOLE WORK

THE object of this book is to expound so-called "Occult Science" upon which rationalist scholars of the present century look with the greatest disdain, considering it as an aberration of the mind of people who are in a low state of mental development, and among whom superstition takes the place of knowledge, and who consider the commonest manifestation of natural laws as a miracle.

This point of view of our learned men, though correct to a certain extent, at the same time shows a very unsatisfactory knowledge of ancient thought and doctrine. Certainly, the ordinary man was in a low state of mental development and was apt to see in almost every event which came under his notice a miracle, produced by some good or evil god. To him, the appearance of the sun, bringing light and heat, was a triumph of the good god over the evil one who reigned during the night in the cold and darkness. To the primitive imagination the different phases of the moon presented an unremitting struggle in which the moon disc was " eaten away " by the enemy ; or on the contrary was " gaining health and strength again." All this concerned the ordinary man of the crowd, who undoubtedly was on a much lower level than he is to-day. Rational Science has educated our children to a degree which allows no place for superstition, and even at school age they know the reason of different natural phenomena and the laws which govern them. So from this point of view contemporary science is right.

But there is another point of view to be considered. It concerns the learned men of antiquity—the " Sages "; the " Initiates."

Observing the monuments which we have inherited from ancient times, we admire the beautiful art, and are astonished by their evident knowledge of the laws of nature. We wonder how, with the primitive means in their possession and their limited experience in building construction, for example, they could have solved such problems in architecture as would be difficult even to a present-day engineer possessing the most modern machinery and tools. All this leads us to conclude that in those ancient times there were men whose knowledge was great, approaching our own and perhaps even in some ways exceeding ours.

Studying the ancient documents, we find a very high development of certain branches of science, e.g. Astronomy. The principles of this ancient knowledge are still at the base of contemporary science, and some of the calculations of the astronomers of ancient Egypt and Chaldea can be confirmed by those of our own learned astronomers.

For example, the precession of Equinoxes and the Zodiacal Year which, according to the Egyptians, corresponded to 25,920 years, up to now is still a debated matter, varying between a little under or over 26,000 years. I repeat that all this ought to be sufficient proof for us that in ancient times there existed men who possessed knowledge equal to or even greater than ours. Where did they learn this knowledge? How could they obtain results which seem difficult even for us? The answer is obvious—in the Temples or so-called Schools of Initiation.

Documents which have reached us from various sources indicate that in these Temples the real knowledge was preserved from the most ancient times, perhaps from the creation of the world. The Holy Scriptures tell us that Moses was an Initiate of the Egyptian Temples, " possessing all their sacred knowledge." Greek philosophers like Plato, Pythagoras, Solon, etc., all certify that the doctrines which they expounded were based upon the science revealed to them in the Temples of Egypt.

Even the Christian Scriptures say : " I called my Son from Egypt," constituting in this symbolic phrase a link between the teaching of Christ and the ancient Egyptian doctrine.

After all these testimonies, the disdain with which our present-day science looks upon the ancient knowledge, particularly upon Occult Science, seems quite unjustified.

To understand the point of view of the ancient scholar-priest, we must put ourselves in his position and study the ancient documents from the point of view of the learned man living among savages. Naturally he could not and would not reveal the secrets of Nature, which would be incomprehensible to the ordinary man, to someone incapable of understanding. He had first to bring him up to a certain stage of psychical development before revealing to him the truth, so that he could understand and profit by that knowledge.

This is the reason why the Schools of Initiation were instituted connected with the Temples, as all science was considered a gift of God and therefore religious. The knowledge taught in these schools was supposed to descend direct from the primitive revelation of the truth to the first man, and it had to be protected so as to retain its purity and not be soiled by unclean hands. That is the reason why all primitive knowledge was occult. The word " Occult " comes from the Latin word " Occultus," which means simultaneously " Secret " and " Mysterious."

All knowledge taught in the ancient Temples was secret, possibly with the object of confining it to segregated groups of men of a certain standard of education. The art of an Architect, of an Astronomer of a Doctor, or of an Embalmer, was " a secret " revealed only to the one who had passed the special training of the Temple. But these arts had nothing mysterious about them, and dealt with the same questions that are openly studied in our Universities.

In addition to these sciences, the Temples taught other branches of knowledge which were hidden under a veil of secrecy and mystery. These branches compose those which we now call " Occult," which present the principles of religion, and a knowledge of the laws of nature, and give Initiates the power to act upon the latter; producing by such action what we might call a miracle. That is why this particular knowledge was carefully kept under " Seven Seals," so that in no case could it fall into the hands of an unworthy person.

In the primitive teaching, the Creation was conceived in the thought of the Creator and executed by His word (the Logos—according to the Greek definition). The echo of this basic teaching is recorded in the Gospel of St. John—" In the beginning was the Word," and in the book of Genesis—" God said (declared His will) ' Let there be light,' and there was light."

According to ancient Egyptian documents (e.g. the stone of Shabaka), the world was conceived in the thought of God, and realised by His tongue. The same idea passes through numerous other hieroglyphic texts. The idea of the Christian Trinity finds its echo in the teaching attributed to Hermes Trismegistus, where it is said that " The Father is the Thought, the Son the Word, and they are united to each other by the vibration of Life."

It is interesting to note here that the Egyptian name corresponding to the Logos of St. John and representing the Word of the Creator by which He executed the act of creation, was " RA," expressed ideographically by " the mouth in action " or in other terms, the mouth proffering the word ! We will return to this when explaining the principles of hieroglyphics.

As I said, the ancient deity called by the Egyptians " Tem " or " Atoum " and in the Bible " Aeloim " (meaning He-the-gods) conceived the Creation in His thought and realised it by His word.

To give the possibility for the different created forms to continue their particular life " According to their kind " (Genesis), a third element was necessarily emanated from the Creator. This element received in the Christian doctrine the name of " Holy Ghost," and in the Hermetic teaching the name of " Life." The latter means that this element contains in itself all the laws necessary to sustain life in all its different manifestations and according to the particular quality of each specimen.

This third principle is qualified in some religious

teachings as the Pro-matter. The Hebraic " Cabala " calls it the " Ish "—the primitive element out of which were created all existing beings as well as all things. The Greeks rendered the same idea by the name " Abussos," by which they translated the word " *Ta-Hom* " employed in the Hebraic text of the book of Genesis. This is translated in the English Bible by the word " Waters." (" The Spirit of God moved upon the face of the waters," Gen. i.) The Ancient Egyptian doctrine personified this element in the name of the god " Nou " who presents simultaneously the mass of primordial water and the laws of nature in a latent state, by which will be produced the differentiation of all created manifestations.

To resume : the third Hypostase of the primitive trinity presents the element upon which God directed His creating power in the form of His Word-Logos. Employing the language of science, we may say that the Logos represents the dynamic power and the " Waters " the static element upon which acts the power of the Word.

As I have made clear, all the ancient teachings, including the Christian Scriptures, agree on the Creation being accomplished by the power of the Word. That is the reason why, in the memory of all the ancient civilisations, there is preserved the reminiscence of a primitive tongue, the words of which had a creative power.

The Bible expresses this idea in the following terms : " God brought the animals in to Adam to see what he would call them ; and whatsoever Adam called every living creature, that was the name thereof " (Gen. ii, 19). The Egyptian text renders the same idea as follows : " Before the creation nothing existed and no one knew the name of any creature." These two examples show the importance of the name given by man in his tongue. The name called a being or thing into actual reality. God created by His omnipotent word, but man gave a name by which the being was realised. In our contemporary languages the pronouncing of the name of a thing creates only the mental representation of it in the imagination. In the primitive language called " Adamic " or " Wattan" the name pronounced correctly produced the effect of realisation.

" A thing exists when it is called by its name," says an Egyptian text, and we see in every tomb and temple the representation in painting or sculpture of meals or various objects which became reality when their names were pronounced. This was called " Per-Khrou "—" The coming to life by the power of the voice."

This peculiarity presents the essential difference between our purely utilitarian languages and the ancient writings, which apart from the phonetic side, indispensable for common use of the tongue, possessed at the same time ideographic and symbolic meanings. These meanings were applied in the name as a sort of mathematical formula which defined the being or thing named.

The knowledge of the correct formula of the name gave to the man either the creating or the destroying power over his fellow men, or over objects that surrounded him. In the following chapters I will give many examples to prove this postulate, as all ancient teaching is based upon this principle and it constitutes also the science called " Magic."

This so much ridiculed ancient science is the one

that teaches the use of the power of the word. Those who laugh at it and consider it as a means of mystification of weak-minded or ignorant men, do not understand its root idea and undervalue its strength. It must be clearly understood that all existing religions, including the Christian religion, employ purely magical proceedings in their ritual. The established prayers, the fumigations and other symbolic acts which constitute the ritual of a religion, are all based upon the belief in the power of the human word and the strength of a certain symbolic act. All this constitutes the science of Magic and therefore we consider the latter as the source of every religion. Those who mock at magic and consider the ancient magician as a charlatan profiting by the stupidity of people, make a great mistake and show their limited knowledge of ancient religions. To understand these, the student must not start his researches with the present-day materialistic point of view, but must try and put himself in the position of the ancient thinkers. Only from this vantage point will he be able to discover the essence of the ancient teaching; and things that at first sight seemed to him purely aberration, will come to reveal a logical and founded reason.

The study of ancient thought must be accomplished by using all the means in our possession : the texts in their phonetic translation; the ideography of the image or of the hieroglyph; and the symbolism attached to every sign and to every object in the picture or to every feature of the architectural monument. One must not forget that the ancient texts (hieroglyphic or Hebrew) possessed facilities that are quite beyond the possibilities of any present-day language.

An idea could be expressed in a way that, to the simple mind, would convey only the ideographic sense of the particular image. For anyone learned merely in writing it would express the idea rendered by the utilitarian wording; but for the adept, the same text or image would unveil the secret of causes and effects, the actual formula of Creation. Heraclitus expressed this triple sense of the Hieroglyphics as : " Speaking, Signifying, and Hiding."

We can say the same thing of the writings of Moses, who received his knowledge in an Egyptian Temple and expressed the doctrines of the Bible in the same triple way. The current translation of the Bible gives only the first, the ordinary or exoteric meaning. Therefore, the many legends which it comprises remain misunderstood, and give to positive science a ready ground on which to contest the value of this eternal book.

This peculiarity of ancient writing renders it impossible for the present-day scholar, approaching the texts only from their grammatical sense, to penetrate into their deeper teaching—in other words, into the essence of the ancient doctrine. Only by careful study of the symbolic and ideographic meanings can one partly unveil the real belief and philosophy which humanity inherited from antiquity.

I say, partly, because it is impossible for a man of the twentieth century, not having been initiated in one of the ancient schools, to understand in its totality the great knowledge of the priests, knowledge which they inherited from the primitive revelation.

This science was strictly protected from the profane in the Temples, constituting what we call the

" Tradition " or the " Cabala," according to the Hebrews, which means literally, " What is given from hand to hand."

The chain of tradition has passed from one Initiate to another, from one civilisation to the following, and the beginning of this chain goes back to the unknown antiquity, passing through the Hebraic scriptures, Assyria, Egypt, and apparently much farther.

Egypt is not the cradle of knowledge, neither is Palestine. The proofs of this are numerous in Egypt and the first is obvious, as every Egyptologist remarks on his first studies of this civilisation. After the Stone Age, in which lived the prehistoric savages in the Nile valley, who did not possess any writing or science and who had the most primitive notion of art, we see suddenly the spreading of a civilisation in full blossom, with a perfect writing, with a developed religion and philosophic system, with an art of a very high standard !

All this could not have been born in Egypt, as in that case we would have seen its gradual development, which, as I said, we cannot trace. The only supposition which we can make is, that it was imported from outside by people who at some time had conquered the savages of the Nile valley. Who were those people ? and from whence did they come ? We can only speculate with more or less proof.

In the present book I will expound my theory on this subject and give proofs which, it seems to me, put it upon a solid basis. The reader will understand from what has been said that the following are indispensable for anyone who would wish to understand the orientation of the ancient thought :

1. A profound study of ancient languages, not only from the phonetic and grammatic point of view adopted by contemporary science, but also of the ideographic and symbolic senses.

2. A study of the symbolism of religious ritual and legends.

3. A study of the so-called Occult Sciences, on which our contemporary wise men look with disdain, but which were considered by the ancients as the greatest accomplishment attainable by man. These sciences bear the names of Magic, Astrology, Numerology, Cabala, Medical Art, etc.

4. For the purpose of understanding the symbolic meaning, the ancient Art will be of great help, for it did not employ ornaments only for the sake of ornamentation or symmetry, but each image, each figure, each object, had a particular meaning and was in its place to reveal the doctrine to that observer who was able to see and understand.

A careful student, by orienting his studies in this direction, will be enabled to reconcile the religious teaching with the discoveries of science. These studies will show him the deep meaning of every myth, of every ritual, and will prove that, for example, the Bible, which in the current translation seems to disagree with the discoveries of science, is really one of the greatest scientific books that has ever been written.

As a result, the discord existing between religion and science will disappear, and man will understand the unique Source of the Creation and the laws full of logic which rule the life which surrounds him.

This knowledge will bring at last real peace on the earth and true fraternity among human beings, working in concert on the way of universal evolution.

PART I

HIEROGLYPHIC WRITING AND PRINCIPLES OF EGYPTIAN RELIGION

CHAPTER I

THE HEIROGLYPHIC LANGUAGE

IN order to be able to bring to light the principles on which the Egyptian religion and philosophic doctrine were based I will present an outline of their system of hieroglyphic writing. As you will understand, this will be only a sketch, as the complete study of the hieroglyphic language represents a whole science and cannot be dealt with in one short chapter. I will therefore content myself by dealing with the subject in general outline and not entering into details. But I hope that this outline will give a sufficiently clear idea of the wonderful skill with which the Egyptians traced in writing their thought, and the extraordinary possibilities which this language possessed. In this way we may be able to understand the reason why the Egyptians were prompted to call their language " the Words of God."

As stated in the introduction, the hieroglyphics contain three significations, which Champollion sensed. He could, however, only interpret one, namely, the most common one. Heraclitus defined them as " speaking, meaning, and hiding." These three significations are phonetic, ideographic, and symbolic.

All writing in its earliest stages was purely ideographic. One does not need to know either how to read or to write to convey a simple idea to one's fellow man by an image. The direct representation by

drawing of an animal or of an object makes it clear
what is meant to be expressed. A picture of a buffalo
under a peculiar tree on a hill would convey the idea
that this kind of game could be found at this particular
spot. The Red-Indians, as well as the savages of
Central Africa, who do not possess any writing, make
themselves understood by their tribesmen by picture
writing. Unconsciously, every one of us began reading in the same way. We give our children either
bricks or books on which are shown pictures to illustrate the letters by which the name of the represented
objects begin, e.g., for H there will be the image of a
house, for D one of a dog, etc.

It is therefore quite obvious that the first writing
was ideographic, but it is interesting to remark that
in the case of the hieroglyphic writing, the ideographic picture, combined with phonetic signs, was
preserved till the end, i.e., when the language had
developed all its complicated grammatical forms.

In all other languages the primitive hieroglyphic
became conventional and the stylographic form
adopted no longer conveys to our imagination the
direct representation of the object. This even applies
to Chinese, which conserved a great number of
hieroglyphics to portray different ideas, which are
still used in their conventionalised form.

With this exception, the evolution in all other
languages took place long ago and the conventional
sign of a letter lost all trace of the primitive hieroglyphic. It would take too long to explain how the
letters have evolved to attain the actual state of our
phonetic language. One example will be sufficient.
In all European languages the letter S or Z presents
a more or less close image of a serpent in movement,

and we can trace it to the ancient Egyptian sign Z and to the hissing sound which this reptile produces.

So the first signification of the hieroglyphic which we must study, is its ideography.

This ideography is of two kinds: Firstly, that which directly portrays an object, and secondly, that which represents the imitation of the sound produced by a living creature.

It is natural that ancient man was struck by the manifestations of nature which surrounded him. The sunrise repeated regularly every day, by its light breaking into the chilly darkness and dispelling its terrors, and the moon in its regular monthly course, attracted the attention of man. He also observed the regular changes of nature during a year or over longer periods, and these observations allowed him to establish a calendar of astronomic cycles among which was the cycle of Sothis or Sirius (Sepdt) of 1461 years, and the cycle of the Zodiacal year composed of 25,920 solar years. All these cycles prove a long observation of astronomical phenomena.

Another feature peculiar to the Nile valley is the regular variation in the height of the water, which made it possible to establish three natural seasons: the flood, the sowing-time, and the harvest. Each of these periods was divided into four months.

The sign of the sun naturally became the sign of the day, as the sign of the moon became that of the month. To denote the year the Egyptians employed the sign of the annual growth of the palm tree.

The glorious sun shining constantly in the cloudless sky impressed greatly the imagination of the ancient Egyptian, and it is natural that from oldest times the sun disc became the principal God, the symbol of light and good, which brought all the necessary elements of life and joy to the earth. The sun became the generating principle, the father of everything and the symbol of constant life in its eternal resurrection.

The signs which evolve from the sun are easily understood: *Akh*, the sun in the horizon at the moment of rising or at the time of setting, symbolising splendour and greatness.

The rising sun *kha*, symbolising the glorious apparition, was applied also to express the Pharaoh ascending to his throne.

Wbn—to shine. *Dy*—to give, represented respectively a hand offering a pyramidal bread or the pyramidal bread itself (without the hand). This sign enters for example into the phrase : " Ra is rising," meaning the gifts that are distributed by the benevolent God to all nature. We can see in Tel-Amarna pictures illustrating this idea in which every ray of the sun disc shining over the Pharaoh ends with a little hand holding in it either the symbol of life, or of gold, or of health, etc.

Another symbol attached to the sun is the face, *Hr*. We read in the religious texts that the sun was symbolised by the human face. This metaphor explains the reason why in the cult of the sun the hawk, *Hor*, became a personification of the sun. This new sign is more complete than that represented by the solar disc only, for it presents the two principal moments of the day. " The sun in the two horizons," or " the two eyes of Horus," implies according to some texts the sun in the east and in the west, and according to other texts the sun and the moon which are at certain times both simultaneously in the sky, like " two eyes of the face of heaven."

We can see the representation of the same idea in the sign of the standard of the east, which is composed of the symbol of light—a twinkling spear on both sides of which are represented two discs symbolising the two eyes of heaven.

Another hieroglyph belonging also to the Sun group is the sign of the course of the disc over the horizon, which phonetically corresponds to the letter *T*. Symbolically, this sign represents the equilibrium, the life which developed between the two moments of birth and death. Grammatically it became the feminine suffix, as for the manifestation of life it is necessary that the masculine principle should be equilibrated by the feminine principle. The union of these two principles gives a possibility of birth to a new life.

This last sign enters into the hieroglyphic symbolising the west, called the west standard, in which we see the vault of the sky and, at one side of it, the feather symbolising the God of light, " Shou." This means that though the sun is dead, having descended under the western horizon, the principle of light is still alive, resulting in the conviction of the imminent resurrection of life. It is interesting to know that the word meaning " to-morrow " was written *bka* and its homonym signified " to expect a child." This shows that the night was considered as a preparatory state, in which the natural forces prepare the imminent birth of the morning sun.

I will stop here in my examples of the signs related to the sun which are very numerous, the sun being the principal element of life. We will proceed to the study of other signs in the sky, which were observed by the ancient Egyptians and played a great role in their religion and mode of life.

The sign of the north in the sky was the constellation of the Great Bear, or the " Thigh " according to the Egyptians. The sign of the " Thigh," as you can observe, reproduces exactly the outline of this constellation. Revolving round the Polar Star, the Thigh was like the hand of a gigantic clock, which marked on the sky the hours of the night. The comprehension of this ancient point of view has allowed me to decipher and understand some very interesting texts, which otherwise had no sense in the accepted and solely phonetic translation.

The star Sirius (or Sothis according to the Greek denomination), called by the Egyptians *Sepdt*, was the morning star, the one which " with long strides prepared the way for the sun." The simultaneous rising of this star with the sun, called the " heliacal rising of Sothis " which happened every 1461 years, gives us a clue to establish some of the dates of Egyptian history, for we find in certain documents the statement, that such and such an event happened when the heliacal rising of Sothis was at such and such a day of such a month.

The evening star, the one which appears first in the western part of the sky after the setting of the sun, is Venus, called *Bennu*, which represents the mythical phœnix " which was born out of the flames." This metaphor becomes comprehensible when one looks at this star appearing in the western part of the sky, inflamed by the sunset rays. A poetic legend refers to Bennu as " the soul of the sun," which appears for a short time in the sky after the death of the god and then rejoins him in the grave to accompany him to the place of his resurrection in the east. In some of the prayers which we read in the

Books of the Dead, the deceased prayed that his soul might become like the Bennu bird and be allowed to join the Sun God in his course in the Under World towards his resurrection on the following morning.

All this concerns the astronomical observations of the Egyptians, but apart from this the latter also observed the life on earth which surrounded them and naturally their attention was primarily attracted by the Nile.

This river forms the artery of the country and brings to the wilderness that water which makes life possible. Without the Nile, Egypt would have remained a desert like its surroundings. The natural course of the river from south to north divided the country into two parts : the east and the west banks called in the texts " the two lands." In other texts we see this description given to Upper and Lower Egypt. This must be explained. The natural and ideal centre of the land of Egypt was Memphis. North of this is the Delta, and south, the upper course of the river beginning at Elephantine or the present Assuan. Though the upper course of the Nile is much longer than the lower part, the latter is wider, but the area it watered north and south was approximately the same. This is the reason why one could say that Memphis, or the " White Wall " joined the " two lands," or in other words the upper course of the Nile and the Delta.

The sign meaning " to join," *sma*, represents the course of the river and the Delta, and one often sees on frescoes two human figures representing the Nile Gods uniting this sign with aquatic plants of Upper and Lower Egypt. This group can also be seen supporting the throne of Pharaoh on frescoes and

c

statues (for example, it is seen on the sides of the thrones of the so-called " Colossi of Memnon ").

I have indicated that the regular changes in the height of the water of the Nile afforded the reason for instituting the division of the year into three seasons. Apart from that, the current flowing from the south to the north was a phenomenon which produced a natural sense of these directions, and the ideographic

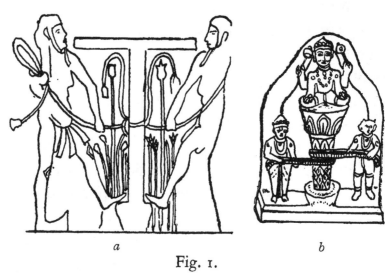

a   *b*

Fig. 1.

(*a*) Egypt. The sign SMA supporting the throne of the Colossus of Memnon; (*b*) India. The god Samudra Mutu. National Museum of New York.

representation of the journey to the north was depicted by a rowing boat, and of the journey to the south by a sailing boat. It was possible to go to the north by descending the current, but it was necessary to hoist a sail to be able to ascend towards the south.

Other signs symbolising these directions were also taken from objects in the Nile valley in the form of aquatic plants : the one of the Delta for the north, and the one of the desert for the south.

" To cross the Nile " from one bank to the other had also a particular significance. The west bank was considered the region of the dead, who " set " in the image of the sun in the west, and we can observe that all the necropoli of ancient Egypt are on the west bank of the Nile and all the towns were on the east bank (with very few exceptions). The funeral procession crossed the Nile in boats going from the east to the west bank like the sun in its daily course in the sky.

Now it is important to say a few words concerning the principal elements of Nature represented by means of hieroglyphic writing and which also have a deep significance in their ideography.

As I have said, the principal element which symbolised the generative force, the masculine principle, was the Sun. It was the symbol of life, of light, and of the active word of God. The name of the Sun God was Râ, meaning " the mouth in action."

The element upon which this action was orientated was the primitive water, which by itself was passive. The sign of passivity is therefore quite naturally given by one representing the surface of the water, which phonetically formed the letter N. It is also the symbol of the horizontal plane. The primitive water was personified in the Egyptian pantheon by the god Nou, the mass of primitive waters, or according to the definition of the book of Genesis, " the waters above and the waters below," before their separation.

The sign opposed to the horizontal plane is the letter B, representing a human leg and symbolising the movement, the elevation from the surface. The words that are inferred by the combination of these two signs are : the first Bn meaning perpendicular, and the second Nb, which expresses the elevation of a surface, and constitutes the name of the basket, Neb, which up to these days we see the women of Egypt lift and carry on their heads.

According to the book of Genesis, the first living creatures on the earth were the reptiles which crawl on the surface, and the Egyptian writing renders the same idea ideographically by the word *fn*, "to crawl." The Egyptian texts relating to the doctrine of the Creation say that the first beings who acclaimed the rising of the sun on the first day of creation were reptiles and this is the reason why the most ancient gods of the pantheon were represented with heads of snakes or lizards.

Man standing upright has elevated himself towards the sky away from the surface, from which he separates himself in every step he takes. This is the reason why the sign of the human leg presents symbolically the idea of elevation. It is also the sign of something hard which " stands upright." For example, to starch a linen cloth, to make it rigid was written *bdt*, representing the action of hardening the cloth which was produced by the human hand.

All the examples that I have given up to now belong to the first group of ideographic signs, namely, those representing the direct image of an object.

The second group is composed of signs, the phonetic sound of which reproduces the particular noise made by an animal which the hieroglyphic represents, or by an inanimate object in motion.

I will just give a few examples of this group to illustrate my statement.

The donkey was read phonetically *yai*, the swallow *wr*, reproducing the sound of its quick flight, the goose was pronounced either *sa* or *gb* in which we hear the typical sound of this bird's voice,

PLATE I.

1. ⊙ Ra, the sun.
   ⊙ Ra - Logos and the sun god.

2. Iah, the moon and Sp - the two lips.

3. Rnp - the annual palm growth.

4. Ah - the sun in the horizon.

5. Kha - the rising sun.
   the act of rising "Book of the Dead" XVII ch. Ra in

6. Wbn - the shining sun

7. Dy - the pyramidal bread. Ra is rising

8. Hr, the face.
   the god Hor, or Horus

9. Ab - the standard of the East

10. Ymn - the standard of the West.

11. Bka - to-morrow.
    " to expect a child.

12. Khpsh or Mskht - the Thigh

13. Bennu, the fabulous phoenix.

14. Sma, to join

15. Khd - to go to the North.

16. Khnt - to go to the South.

17. Mh - plant of the Delta, the North

18. Shmâ - plant of the desert - the South.

19. Bn - the perpendicular Ben-ben - the Pyramidion.

20. Nb, the basket.

the lion was pronounced *rw*, characterising the roaring of this beast, and the cat was the sign for *miu* or *mau*.

It is interesting to follow the development of the symbolic meaning of some of these hieroglyphics. For example, the word *miu* represented ideographically by the image of the cat, symbolically meant " to be like " or " the image of."

In the seventeenth chapter of the Book of the Dead (reproduced for example in the tomb of Queen Nefertari) we see a fresco representing a big cat in the act of cutting with a knife the head of a great serpent. The text which accompanies this picture says : " The male cat is Ra himself and he is called Mau by reason of the speech of the god Sa (the god of wisdom) who said concerning him : *he is like* (Mau) *unto that which he hath created*—thus his name became Mau."

This sibylline statement gives us a clue which explains the combination of the two significations in the hieroglyphic writing. The unlearned man understood this picture in its most simple and direct form : it only conveyed to his intelligence the idea of a cat attacking a serpent. But the Initiate understood the same representation in its symbolic meaning, which was that the Creation was accomplished according to the *law of similarity ;* an idea which is expressed in the Bible by the words : " God created man in His Own Image, in the Image of God created He him " (Gen. i, 27).

The image of the swallow in its symbolic sense signifies " greatness," multitude ; conveying the idea of the development of the primitive unity into infinite parts for the purpose of all the numerous individual manifestations in Creation. The name of the Creator

is accompanied in the religious texts by two epithets :
aâ and *wr*, both meaning " great." But the first
epithet concerns greatness by elevation and can be
defined as the synthetic greatness of the Unity. This
epithet accompanies also the name of the Pharaoh to
express his greatness, his elevation, over all other
men. The second epithet signifies the greatness of
division, the analytic greatness of the Principle in its
infinite manifestations. In other words, these two
epithets represent the Creator as the infinitely big as
well as the infinitely small ; the beginning and the
end, or according to the Apocalypse of St. John :
" the Alpha and Omega," and according to the
Hebraic doctrine : " Aleph and Tau," the first and
the last letters of the alphabet.

The separate parts of the body of the lion, *rw*, had
also symbolic as well as ideographic significations.
The front part, *ht*, in its direct sense meant " front,"
and in its abstract sense, " the chief," " the better,"
" the prince " ; and concerning the human body—
" the heart," which the Hebraic Cabalists define as
" the king (Melek) of the body."

The hind-quarters, *hk*, represented "force," vigour,
expressing the vigorous movement which they gave
to the animal. Symbolically this sign meant " supernatural power," magic force, and thus composed the
name of the god of Magic, *Heka*.

I have to stop here in dealing with the ideographic
and symbolic meanings, and will proceed to sketch
the phonetic or grammatical sense of the language.

When primitive thought attained to a certain state
of development, and it was required to express
abstract ideas and render them in complicated grammatical forms of speech, the direct ideographic

representation of an object became insufficient, and it was necessary to create a phonetic writing elastic enough to express the different shades of human thought.

First of all, to show that an abstract meaning had to be given to a word, the Egyptians accompanied it with the sign of the sealed book, which at once conveyed the idea that the word was not to be taken in its direct ideographic sense.

Twenty-six signs were then chosen represented by the most simple objects: birds, or features of the human body. These signs became phonetic sounds just like our letters, and entered into the structure of the different words, as well as into the composition of grammatical forms. But these phonetic letters did not replace altogether the ancient ideographic signs, but were only combined with them to form the phonetic framework of different words, as well as the necessary endings, to render possible the expression of grammatical forms.

These were not simply imagined, but deduced from the primitive symbolic meaning of the particular sign.

Thus the snail, which became the letter *F*, was grammatically " *He,*" symbolising the first living being, the reptile which was born at the Creation and which, as the texts say, " acclaimed the first apparition of the sun."

The sign of the surface of water became phonetically the sound *N* and grammatically formed the past participle, symbolising by this that the action had stabilised itself, was congealed, had no more movement.

The sign of the chicken gave the sound *W* or *U* and grammatically formed the pronoun " *I,*" symbolising a living creature which realises its particular existence.

It is interesting to note here that the verb " to be,"

PLATE II

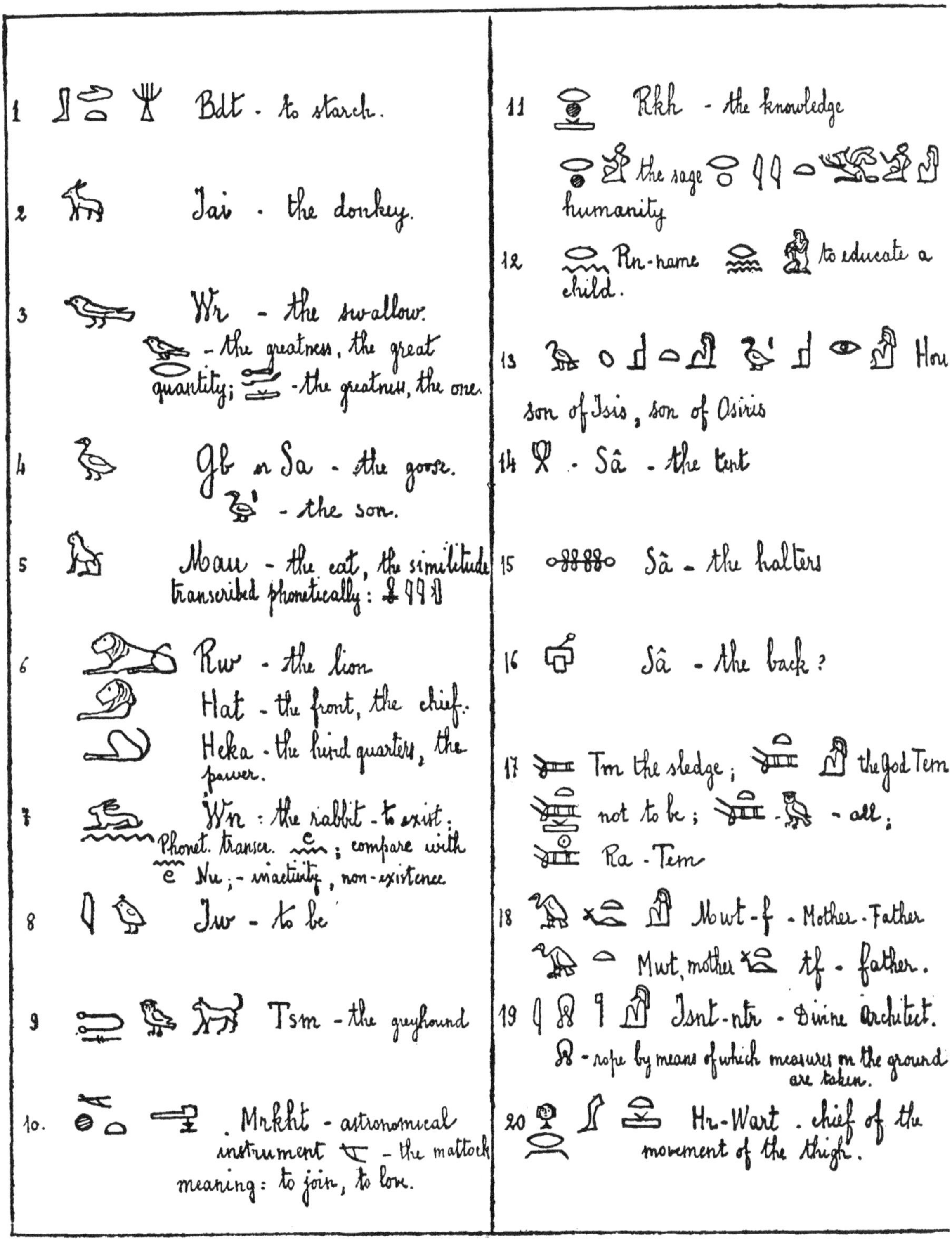

1. Bdt - to starch.

2. Iai - the donkey.

3. Wr - the swallow.
   - the greatness, the great quantity; - the greatness, the one.

4. Gb or Sa - the goose.
   - the son.

5. Mau - the cat, the similitude transcribed phonetically:

6. Rw - the lion
   Hat - the front, the chief.
   Heka - the hind quarters, the power.

7. Wn : the rabbit - to exist.
   Phonet. transcr. ; compare with Nu ; - inactivity, non-existence

8. Iw - to be

9. Tsm - the greyhound

10. Mrkht - astronomical instrument - the mattock meaning: to join, to love.

11. Rkh - the knowledge
    the sage humanity

12. Rn - name to educate a child.

13. Hou son of Isis, son of Osiris

14. Sâ - the tent

15. Sâ - the halters

16. Sâ - the back ?

17. Tm the sledge ; the god Tem
    not to be ; - all ;
    Ra - Tem

18. Mut-f - Mother-Father
    Mut, mother tf - father.

19. Isnt-ntr - divine architect.
    - rope by means of which measures on the ground are taken.

20. Hr-Wart . chief of the movement of the thigh.

Iw, was written by the sign of the chicken preceded by the one of the papyrus stems, by which the scribe traced the hieroglyphics.

In ancient Hebrew the principal letter is *Iod*, which represents the manifestation of the unity of God (numerically the number 10) and enters physically into the construction of every letter of the alphabet. In the Egyptian hieroglyphics the same phonetic sound " *I* " is represented by the stem of papyrus, by the means of which the scribe traced all the signs, rendering visible, or in other words materialising, " the words of God." As you can see, the idea is practically the same.

In the verb " to be," which we discuss, the combination of the being (chicken), which realises its existence and proclaims its individuality—" I myself " is realised in its particular form by means of the papyrus stem, which has traced the image of the being, rendering it real, existing materially.

What is remarkable and shows the extraordinary logic of the primitive conception, is that in old days the letter *I*, representing the pen, was replaced by the letter *R*, representing the mouth and symbolising the creating word, the Logos. Thus " the word of God " (*Ra*) fixed by the writing was rendered visible in the written language by the substitution of the sign of the pen (*I*) for the sign of the Logos (*R*). This seems to correspond textually to the statement of the Gospel of St. John : " And the word became flesh."

Another word meaning also " to be," to " exist," was *wn*, represented by a rabbit sitting on the sign of the surface. Phonetically this word is transcribed by the letters *W*, the spiral, and *N* the surface, combined thus *WN*.

I draw your attention to the ideography of this phonetic word, in which the spiral symbolises the constructive laws of nature placed *over the sign of the surface*. To exist in reality everything had to come out " *over the surface*," at the image of the sun which " appeared above the surface of the primordial waters," creating by this act the beginning of life on the earth. As I have said, the name of the god personifying the pro-matter as well as the forces of nature in a latent state, was *Nw*, showing ideographically the spiral of natural forces *under the surface* of the waters, or in other words, in a state of inactivity.

I think that these few examples are sufficient to show that, even in its phonetic transcription, the hieroglyphic writing preserved the ideographic sense expressed by the particular disposition of the signs.

In the phonetic alphabet, there exist a few double signs which express the same sound. These signs are for *S*, the lock, and the *Candlet*, in which the mummy was enveloped as well as the new-born child.

The first was the symbol of stability, of the locking of a thing in a precise state ; and the second—the symbol of the eternity of life in its changes from birth to death, which in its turn will again produce a new birth.

For the sound *T*, I have already explained the significance of the sign of the sky vault. The other sign represents a bola employed by huntsmen to catch an animal. Its symbolic meaning expresses the holding together of things by force, an intervention from the outside.

For *W* or *U* the signs, as I have said already, were the chicken and the spiral, the first relating to the microcosmos and the second to the macrocosmos, representing the natural forces in action.

I have outlined the particular ideas conveyed by these signs.

For the sound *M* one hieroglyph represents an owl, the night bird, opposed to the eagle, the bird of the sun which renders the sound *A*.

As the eagle is the symbol of spirituality and of life conveyed by the idea of the glorious day—the owl is the one of darkness, of death, and of matter. It is logical from this point of view that grammatically this latter sign was used as the preposition " in," expressing an envelopment in matter, in darkness.

The other sign for the sound *M* showed the joining of the two different planes, " the waters above with the waters below " according to the Bible. This sign was the prototype that created the Hebraic and the Samaritan letters *Mem*, which has got the same symbolic meaning.

The grammatical sense attributed to this hieroglyphic is " with " showing the natural joining of two elements.

For the sound *H*, we have also two signs, one showing the plan of a material construction, the application by man of the natural forces expressed in the case of the macrocosmos by the sign of the spiral.

The other sign represents a rope with three loops, expressing the idea of something bound or lifted (for example, to elevate and fix the mast of a boat). In a deeper sense this sign means the joining of the three planes constituting the human being.

The Egyptian language possessed a sound unknown in modern tongues, which can be rendered approximately by *KH*. This sound was represented also by

Sign	Phonetic Meaning	Ideographic Meaning.	Symbolic Meaning	Grammatical Meaning.
	A	Eagle	Spiritual part, the light.	
	B	The human leg.	Vertical movement, rigidity.	
	D	The human hand.	Human work, to take, to intervene.	
	G	The Pylon of the temple.	To cover, to hide.	
	F	The snail.	First manifestation of individual life.	pronoun "he".
	H	The rope.	To lift, to tie.	
	"	The plan of a building.	Application of human work, to bend.	
	K	The mason's basket in which he carries and mixes sand and cement	A vase, a shell, which separates a particular mixture from the mass of material.	pronoun "thou".
	Kh	A sieve.	The mixture of elements, the combination.	
	"	The womb.	The organ in which is formed the body of the child	
	M	The owl.	The darkness, the envelopment, the matter.	preposition: "in".
	"	Two parts of a thing	The natural joining of two parts (e.g. of the matter above and the matters below).	preposition "with"
	N	The surface of water.	Horizontal plane, passiveness.	With a verb: Past Tense. With a noun: Dative Case.

two signs to express the macrocosmic or abstract ideas and the microcosmic, purely human effect. The first sign represents a sort of sieve through which the rough matter was passed and purified (for example sand or cement), before it could be employed for building. Abstractly this sign related to a particular combination : a mixture of elements necessary to produce a determined manifestation.

The other sign represented conventionally the womb of the mother, in which was formed the body of the child.

In the texts right from those first known to us, i.e. those of the Pyramids, and to the end of the Egyptian civilisation, we see phonetic letters and ideographic signs simultaneously entering into the composition of the words. The reason for this was that some of these signs could not be replaced by phonetic letters without altering the symbolic and ideographic sense of the word. Also we see a word written in phonetic letters accompanied by an ideographic representation of its meaning. Such a sign accompanying the word is usually called the " determinative," and the reason for its employment is to make precise the sense of the phonetic word as there existed many homonymous words, the respective meanings of which were often different.

I will give here just a few examples so that these ideas may be quite clear.

The Greyhound was denominated by the phonetic sounds *tsm*, the determining sign being the picture of the precise kind of dog. The signs entering in the phonetic composition of this name were : the bola, meaning " to capture," to catch, to join ; the lock, signifying that the animal caught was " held firmly " ;

and the owl, pointing to the fact that the word concerned a material thing, was enveloped " in " a material effect.

We see in some texts the representation of an astronomical instrument the precise nature of which unfortunately has not yet been discovered, i.e. we do not know what material purpose it served. It was called *mrkht*, signifying that it joined (*MR*, the sign of the hoe, which joined together the particles of earth, covered the grain which was sown, and abstractly signified " to love," the feeling that joins two beings), a precise combination in the sky. The determining sign pictures clearly enough a kind of telescope on a revolving support.

The following is an example of the evolution of an idea expressed by means of hieroglyphic writing. *Rkh* signifies " knowledge," showing graphically the creating Word acting upon a combination. The wise man, the sage, was written *rkh*, and the humanity *rkhit*, showing that every man can become wise, for he is endowed for this purpose with all the necessary elements : the creating word which can form a precise combination. The representation of a fabulous bird that accompanies this last word expresses, according to Egyptian convention, the soul which differentiates the man from any other living being.

The " name " of a man was rendered by the word *rn*, showing ideographically the creating word above the surface of primordial water, or in other terms, " the fixed action of the Logos." And to educate a child was written *rnn*, showing in the determinative sign the picture of the mother nursing her child, and in the phonetic formation, the addition to " the name " *RN* of a second *N*, sign of the surface. This can be interpreted as the solid foundation upon which the name given to a child rests, or in other words his education in the traditions and principles of the particular family, which will make out of him a worthy member, who will bear his name with honour.

I will stop here in giving examples in the fear of fatiguing the reader. I hope that I have made sufficiently clear the principles of hieroglyphic writing. I must only add that the so-called " determinative signs " which we see in nearly all ancient texts, are missing in the magical texts, as, for example, those of the Pyramids. The reason was that the Egyptians believed that the image traced ideographically could be revived and given a real life by the power of magic. This was called, as I mentioned in the introduction, " the calling to life by the power of the voice " (*Per-Khrou*).

The reason why in magical texts the ideographic sign was missing, was to restrict only to the initiate the use of the formula in evoking to life the named elements or beings. The simple man of the crowd would not understand without the determinative sign to what order of ideas the text he read had reference.

Sometimes also we see in these texts images representing noxious creatures, as for example serpents, lions, scorpions, etc. (which had to be employed in the formation of the words), pierced by knives, or cut in half, or with their legs cut off. The explanation is also obvious : in the case of someone, not having the necessary knowledge, succeeding in evoking to life one of these dangerous beings, they could not injure him or anyone else, as they had been paralysed previously by the magician, who traced their images.

To conclude, I will give an example of homonymous

PLATE IIIB

Sign	Phonetic Meaning	Ideographic Meaning	Symbolic Meaning.	Grammatical Meaning
℮	U, W	The spiral.	Universal forces in action.	
🐤	" "	The chicken	Individual body.	Pronoun: "myself"
□	P	The cubic stone.	Equilibrated formation, as a result of the work of man.	
△	Q	A heap of sand.	Shapeless matter, prepared to be transformed by man.	
⬭	R	The mouth.	A gate, the Logos.	Primitive sign for the verb to be.
ſ	S	The bandlet of the mummy's swattings	To envelop, to force an action on somebody.	Femin. pronoun: "She"
+	'	The lock.	To fix something in a precise state.	
⌓	T	The vault of the sky.	Cycle developing between life and death, equilibrium.	
⟿	"	The bola	To join two things by force, to capture.	Possessive pronoun: "thine"
۹	Y, I	The papyrus stem, the pen which traces all the signs.	Manifestation of the creative principle.	Pronoun: "I."
⌐	Â	The arm.	The action.	
∿	Z	The serpent.	Eternal life.	
⊡	Sh	The lake with the way of the ferry boat across.	The accumulation of promatter.	

D

signs which, though having all the same phonetic value, possessed in each case a different but precise meaning. The phonetic value of all the following signs is *sa*.

The first represents a goose, and apart from its ideographic meaning, with a little stroke it was employed in titulary phrases to express the idea of " son of so-and-so." We meet this expression in all the historic documents describing the descendants of the Pharaoh or of the simple man.

The sign of the egg had got the same phonetic value and symbolically also meant " the son." The difference between these two denominations is, that the first concerned a real being actually existing, " the son—natural heir of his father." The second expresses the idea of conception—the son who was " conceived in the body of his mother," but not yet born. It is natural that this second sign was not employed in documents concerning the descendants of human beings actually existing. It is used sometimes to describe the descendants of gods, who do not actually exist as realities. For example, in one text we see the two different signs (the goose and the egg) employed respectively. And I translate this text : " Horus the son conceived by Isis, the heir of Osiris."

Then come three different signs with the same phonetic *Sa*, which are all usually translated by the word " protection," though it is quite clear that each one of them had a particular meaning.

The first represented a cover, a hood, perhaps the symbolic " skin," or ritual robe by being enveloped in which the Egyptian believed that strength and youth could be renewed. Thus it can be rendered as meaning : " the magical intervention to revive the fading forces."

The second sign represents shackles, with which men were fettered or cattle are tied. The symbolic meaning of this sign becomes quite clear when one studies the ancient pictures and texts concerning the funeral ritual. One sees in the sun temple of Abou-Gourab the representation of men forming groups by holding each other by the hands to constitute a chain, and texts found in some tombs (for example, the one of Rekh-Mara), say about this moment of the ritual that " those surrounding him (the deceased) would form a sympathetic chain of influence for the elevation of the deceased." Thus this particular sign expresses the idea of a magnetic chain formed for the sake of emanating a certain current necessary for a precise magical manifestation, in the same way as the method adopted by spiritualists in their sittings at the present day.

The object represented by the last sign, *Sa*, is difficult to define, but its meaning seems to concern " the back," and the texts say that " the magic power comes (or is radiated) through the back." This is quite in accordance with the latest discoveries of science, which considers the grey matter in the backbone as the centre emanating the nervous fluid.

I will stop my examples here, as I am afraid that I have taxed the attention of the reader, but I hope that what I have said will prove sufficient to convince him as regards the views I have expressed.

A deeper study of this subject demands much time, and many would not be sufficiently interested in this particular branch of knowledge to pursue the matter farther. However, this general outline will have an important bearing on the succeeding chapters.

CHAPTER II

THE PRINCIPLE

THE generally accepted opinion concerning the Egyptian religion is that it is essentially pantheistic. This opinion is based on the fact that we see numerous statues of different deities as well as an infinite procession of gods and goddesses, every one bearing a separate name and apparently playing a particular role. We see them represented in frescoes and on carvings on the walls of temples and tombs. Our opinion therefore seems to be well based, and it is generally considered that Moses was the first who instituted the monotheistic religion and forbade the adoration of idols.

But a deeper study of the Egyptian religion proves that this generally accepted opinion is not quite correct, and beneath the vulgar form of idol worship we can observe a deeper abstract idea. As I have said, the mass of people in ancient Egypt were in a low state of mental development and were not ready to understand abstract ideas. Therefore the creation of a pantheon composed of concrete divinities, some good and some evil, but every one possessing particular attributes, was necessary. The Bible gives us proofs that when Moses absented himself for a short time from his people they at once made themselves idols. They were not prepared to understand the abstract idea of God—the Creator of everything, the Reason that conceived the Universe and that ruled over all the smallest manifestations of life, but remained unseen and could not be understood by man. It took a long time for Moses to introduce and establish the idea of monotheism in the conception of his people, and even after his time, though they accepted the new religion, they could not understand and still less explain it. The idea of God remained for them as something vague, of which they could only sense certain qualities.

I have explained in the preceding chapter how in the hieroglyphic writing the initiate could combine three different significations, which rendered it possible for the unlearned men to understand certain exterior principles regarding the ideas conveyed by the ideographic signs. But the same signs were understood differently by the initiate, to whose mind they conveyed explanations of the deepest philosophical nature.

The same thing can be said about the religion. The exterior part of it intended for the mass of primitive people was simple and concrete, representing different forces of nature under the form of the different divinities forming the Pantheon.

But the man of learning, the initiate, saw in these gods the incarnation of an abstract idea, one of the infinite manifestations of the Creative Power of the Sole Reason which was at the beginning and which conceived and gave birth to the whole Universe with all its infinite species of beings.

That the man of learning in Egypt never believed that the idol was in reality a God, we can judge from the following statement, which we inherited from the remotest times of the Old Kingdom.

" One generation passeth on to another among men, and God, who knoweth character, hath hidden Himself. He is One who confoundeth by what is seen of the eye. Let God be served in His fashion, whether made of precious stone or fashioned of copper, like water replaced by water. There is no stream that suffereth itself to be hidden ; it bursteth the dyke by which it was hidden." This remarkable utterance of an Egyptian thinker of over 4000 years ago, says Professor Breasted, is obviously an effort to distinguish between the god and the conventional temple image which comes forth in the temple procession and is acclaimed by the multitude. But as " water bursts the dyke," so the being of God cannot be confined within the visible image.

This wonderful statement seems to afford sufficient proof of the real conception of the ancient man of learning, and though, as we see, the Egyptian religion is pantheistic in its appearance, the idea of One God, the Creator of everything, passes like a red thread through the whole teaching from the most ancient times of the Pyramid texts right on to the end of ancient Egyptian civilisation. This God was named *Tem* or *Atoum*, and his name was written by the sign of the sledge.

I will explain this sign, which at the first sight does not convey to our conception anything material and might seem purely conventional.

In old days a vehicle on wheels was not employed in Egypt. The battle-chariot drawn by horses appears only in the times of the XVIIIth dynasty. Before the Egyptians entered into intercourse with their neighbours and conquered all the known world, they did not need any kind of vehicle, as all communication in the country was carried on by means of the Nile, either going upstream (to the south) for which a boat was used with sail hoisted, or downstream (to the north) when oars were used. People of a certain standing, as for example the Pharaoh and officers of the State, were carried by slaves in palanquins from their palaces to the bank of the river, where they got into boats.

All heavy material for constructions including statues of divinities were placed, for transport by land,

Fig. 2.
The statue placed upon the sledge. Tomb of
Peta-Amen-Ap.

on sledges. This vehicle became a conventional sign for movement, and even the image of a god who was carried in a procession, was *placed on a sledge* to indicate movement, or more correctly, the principle of movement. To represent the daily course of the sun, for example, the symbolic boat in which the disc was supposed to navigate the waters of heaven was placed on a sledge and dragged round the sanctuary.

The image of a god appearing in a procession was adored, but *the reason of this appearance*—the sledge— was passed unobserved.

Thus the deeper meaning of the ideographic

representation of the sledge can be defined as " the reason of movement," or in other words " the reason of life."

We understand, therefore, that the representation of the name of the Creator, *Tem*, by the hieroglyphic of the sledge is appropriate and illustrates the deep and philosophic thought of the ancient initiate.

But this is not all. The same word, *tem*, with the sign of an abstract idea means " not to exist," or in other words, " not to have a material and particular form." This second meaning is also very informative and represents the Creator as the mysterious reason, the abstract idea which cannot have and does not require a concrete representation. This accords perfectly with the teaching of the Christian catechism, which can only describe certain qualities of God, but cannot define Him.

The third meaning of the same word, *tem*, to which is added the sign of the owl (expressing, as you remember, the material manifestation, or the preposition " IN "), is " ALL." This means that all the manifestations of the visible world have come into being from the one Source of creation, or in other words, that though God has not got a particular form—*He is in all the forms of His creation*.

You see how by employing only one appropriate sign the ancient initiate could render in hieroglyphic language the deepest inner meaning which had to be expressed in later languages in long philosophic treatises.

The texts say that before the Creation, " Tem lived alone in the Nou." As you remember, the *Nou* was simultaneously a personification of pro-matter (the primordial mass of waters), and the symbol of inactivity.

The Bible renders the same idea in the following words: "And the Spirit of God moved on the face of the waters."

The Egyptian teaching can be interpreted in two ways: the first corresponds to that expressed in the Bible as it is said that "Tem lived alone in the primitive waters."

The second meaning is, that before the first movement giving rise to Creation, God was *in a state of inactivity*.

It is important to remark here that the Egyptian doctrine did not indicate a belief in two different sources at the beginning of the Creation, as we might deduce erroneously from the text mentioned. No, other texts state definitely that *Nou* (the pro-matter) was created by Tem, so as to provide the necessary element out of which would be developed all the different forms of the Universe.

Creation was accomplished by God by means of proffering His Word, or Order, which gave the first shock to the inertness and called to life the constructive forces of nature.

The Bible, including the Gospels, express the same idea in the same words: "God said: let there be light—and there was light"—the effect and realisation of the word of the Creator is immediate. And according to the Gospel of St. John, "in the beginning was the Word (Logos)."

In the Egyptian texts it is said: "Ra rose in the beginning."

I have explained above that the name of the god Ra signified simultaneously "the sun" and the "active word."

One understands therefore the wonderful double

meaning that was expressed in the ancient legend which says that "the world began when the sun appeared for the first time over the surface of the waters." In the symbolic sense this means that the world began when God proffered His creating word and thus broke the silence of inactivity.

The " word " (*Logos*) appears under a form of reality in the solar disc, which rose over the world and started to distribute its gifts. (" And the word became flesh.")

But the same hieroglyphic text gives another and yet stronger precision to the role of the *logos*.

The sign *khâ* representing the rising of the sun, apart from its direct meaning, has got another abstract sense which is " tool," or " instrument."

Thus the statement: " Ra rose "—can be interpreted—" the word of God was the tool," by the means of which was accomplished the Creation.

In the texts of the Pyramids we find the name *Tem-Ra,* in which the sign of the sledge is combined with that representing the sun's disc.

This double name defines God in His two different phases: the hidden reason of the Creation and its visible manifestation.

The Hebraic Cabala gives a wonderful definition of the same idea in the following words: " The divine image is double; it consists of the head of light and of the head of shade. . . . He (the manifested God corresponding to the Egyptian god Ra) is the light, but it is the dark head (corresponding to the Egyptian god Tem) which is the lamp."

So the first act of the Creator was to divide the primitive unity into two, which is rendered in the Egyptian texts by the epithet of Tem: *Mout—F.*

This word is a combination of two words: *Mout* meaning " mother," and *Tef* meaning " father." They are joined indivisibly together by the sign of the equilibrium, showing by this that the two opposite principles (feminine and masculine) are in potentiality in God, the sole Cause of everything, *Who is simultaneously the Father and the Mother of all beings.*

The Hebraic Cabala rendered the same idea, saying, that before the Creation " the Balance was in the Eternal Being." And Pythagoras expresses the same basical principle as follows: " The Great Monad acts in the creating Dyad. At the moment that God manifests Himself He becomes double: the indivisible essence and the divisible substance; the masculine principle which is active and the feminine principle which is passive, or in other words the animated and plastic matter. Thus the Dyad represents the union of the eternal masculine and the eternal feminine in God; the two essential divine faculties."

Orpheus expressed the same idea in the following verse: " Jupiter is the husband and the divine wife."

In the Vedas the Creator is compared to a spider, " the Father-Mother unrolls the cobweb, the upper end of which is attached to the spirit—light in the darkness; and the lower end is attached to the dark extremity—matter. And this cobweb is the Universe which unrolls outside the two principles combined in one."

And another Vedic text says: " The Father-Mother is the graphic name given to the Eternal when He is considered in the act of making the universe emanate out of His own essence."

We find the same idea expressed in identical words to those of the Egyptian text in the doctrine of the

Maya civilisation of South America, which calls God " the First, the Mother and the Father of all beings, the cause of existence, the Creator of every thing."

Examples which present the same idea in different religious doctrines could be extended indefinitely.

Those given are sufficient to illustrate the point.

As you will observe, the principle of division of the primitive Unity was considered in all ancient religious teachings as fundamental, being that which rendered possible the manifestation of life.

According to the book of Genesis all Creation was produced by God following the same principle of division : to light was opposed darkness ; to the sky (the waters above)—the terrestrial plane (the waters below) ; to the principle of humidity (water)—that of dryness (earth), and so on.

The Christian Trinity constitutes precisely the same principle of division of the unity in two opposed elements, which must be equilibrated, one with the other. The point of equilibrium which constitutes the mutual relation between the two opposed principles is the natural third hypostasis of the Christian Trinity.

In a typical pagan trinity the three elements that compose it are : the father, the mother, and the child born from the union of the two parents.

I shall presently give examples of different pagan trinities which are all built upon the same principle of a divine family.

What is important to remember is that the principle of division was, according to the teaching of all ancient religions, *in the Unity of the Creator* in a latent state. (" The Balance in the body of the Eternal " according to the Hebraic Cabalists, or " the Mother-

Father," the epithet of the Creator employed in Egyptian and other teachings.)

The modern scientist, observing the mystery of the conception of life, remarks that it develops itself in consecutive divisions: the ovum, being fecundated, divides itself into two, into four, into eight, and so on, to arrive at last at the formation of the body of a being constituted of an innumerable quantity of cells.

A text of the Egyptian teaching says: "I am one who became two, I am two who became four, I am four who became eight—but I am One who protects all."

The meaning of this sibylline statement is clear after what was said concerning the basic principle of the Egyptian doctrine, and it can be rendered thus: "Though for the manifestation of different forms of life the One Cause had to divide itself into innumerable forms, it stays nevertheless One and Unchangeable," or in other words, the same primal Cause, by penetrating into all and everyone of the smallest divisions of Creation, maintains life in all its different manifestations.

I subsequently explain how the development of the idea of the division gave rise to the numerous gods of the Pantheon in the ideographic system of the Egyptian teaching.

Now I will give some epithets of the Creator which accompany His name in different Egyptian texts and define His role and His quality. These epithets have received interesting interpretations in different religious teachings, which were developed out of the Egyptian doctrine.

There are two epithets usually applied to Tem, both translated by Egyptologists as "Great." As

I have explained, the first expresses the synthetic greatness of the unity containing in potentiality all the manifestations to be; the second concerns the analytic greatness of the innumerable beings of the created world.

Tem is often called "the one of millions of years," represented ideographically either by a man with hands elevated to the sky, in the conventional pose of adoration and having a stem of a palm annual growth on his head, or by the picture of the god himself

Fig. 3.

The god Tem, tomb of Queen Nefertari.

holding in his hand a palm stem covered with numerous growths. The Hebraic Cabalists call the Creator "Ain-Soph," which means literally, "the Ancient of years."

Other texts present Tem as the "Divine architect," representing this word by the ideographic sign of the coiled rope by means of which the architect traced and measured on the ground the plan of the construction.

Plato expresses the same idea when he calls God "the eternal Geometer and the Supreme Artist whose work is the Universe."

Sometimes Tem is called " the soul of souls "—a meaning that is quite clear and does not need any explanation.

In yet another epithet Tem was called " the chief of the movement of the Thigh." I said in the first chapter that the Thigh was the name of the constellation of the Great Bear, and that its revolving movement round the north point in the sky was like the motion of the hand of a clock. But all the apparent movement of the sky is effected round the same point. Thus " the chief," or " the centre " of the movement of the Thigh will naturally be the centre of the sky, or in other words—of the whole visible world. One of the books comprising the Hebraic Cabala, the Sepher Ietzirah, states :

" The Dragon is in the centre of the sky like a king on his throne." It is important to know that from 3500–2000 years before Christ the Polar Star was the Alpha of the constellation of the Dragon. Thus " the King on his throne," around whom passes daily all the innumerable court of the stars, is another poetic form of defining the role of the Creator.

I hope that these few examples I have given will be sufficient to illustrate the idea of the ancient doctrine concerning the Supreme Cause of the Creation, and that the reader understands that it was far deeper and more philosophical than the simple pantheistic religion which presents only its exterior aspect.

CHAPTER III

THE VERB

YOU will remember that the creative word in the hieroglyphic language was *RA*, written by the sign of the " mouth " and the one of the " arm," and meaning literally the " mouth in action." This word was at the same time the name of the sun god, and was represented ideographically by the conventional sign of the sun disc.

The word of God once proffered became a reality, or in other words, became visible. One understands, therefore, that the name *RA* was appropriate to the solar disc, which was the source of all life on the earth and at the same time the centre of light which rendered visible all the forms of creation.

It is interesting to follow the development of this idea. The sign which expressed the idea " to create " was " YR," representing the eye. A thing once created became visible, and therefore the image of the eye to render the idea of a formation in reality is comprehensible and logical.

We read in the Bible, concerning the creation of elements and beings, the following sentence : " And God saw that it was good." This sentence ends every accomplished act of the Creator which preceded the creation of man. Concerning man it is said in the Bible : " And the Lord God formed man of the dust of the ground " (Gen. ii, 7).

These two ways of expressing the Creation seem to be taken by Moses straight from the Egyptian teaching, where it is said that God " created (*saw*) the *Nou* (pro-matter), created (*saw*) the earth and *fashioned* humanity " (papyrus Hu Nefer Hymn to the sun).

I have explained the meaning of the sign *YR* (the eye)—" to contemplate the visible effect of the manifestation of the creating power."

The word *QMA*—to fashion, used in the text in regard to the creation of man, is formed by the sign *Q*, representing a heap of matter without shape which must be transformed by the action either of God or of man into a precise form. The sign *MA* represents a sickle and its symbolic meaning is " rightfulness, truth." It can be thus interpreted here as expressing correct action applied to the shapeless matter which will render it harmonious and beautiful. The result of all the Creation of God is beautiful, as on the contrary a shapeless thing, or a disharmonic noise can never present the deed of a real artist.

The sign that determines the word that we analyse represents the boasting chisel with which the sculptor fashioned the rough material and made out of it a perfect object of art.

So in the mentioned hieroglyphic passage we see a very interesting combination of signs by means of which is rendered the idea of the creation of man— the masterpiece of the Great Artist. And, as I said, in this short sentence we easily trace the genesis of the idea expressed by Moses in the Book of Creation.

The name employed in the mentioned text to define humanity was explained in the preceding chapter and shows graphically the reasonable being, the one possessing the word and capable himself of composing a precise combination.

This name is accompanied by the representation of a mythical bird which shows that the being in question is provided with a soul, or, in other words, that the physical formation, "out of the dust," does not constitute the whole of man, but that an important part of him presents a spiritual being.

The word YR—" to create, to see," was employed concerning the action either of God or of man (the image of God), the reasonable being. When one wanted to express the idea "to look" in general concerning man as well as any animal species provided with eyes, one employed another sign, MAA, representing the sickle and the two retina—the physical "windows" of an animal body by the means of which the living being received the balanced impression of the material world surrounding it.

As you can understand, there is a great difference between these two signs, expressing the same idea "to see." The first, YR, concerns the impression of a reasonable being contemplating the result of his own work—"I have created this and I look and judge if the work of my hand is good or not."

The second word, MAA, can be translated "to look." This does not necessitate the reasonable contemplation, but only the fact of reflection of an object in the physical organ which is the eye.

One will understand, therefore, the thought which the Egyptian initiate wanted to convey to our reason by expressing the verb "to create" by the hieroglyphic of the eye.

It is curious to remark here that in many coloured frescoes in tombs we see the sign of the eye when it expresses the idea " to create " painted externally in blue, but having the retina red. On the contrary, in the case when the image of the eye concerns this organ or its faculty " to look "—the whole of the eyes is painted either in blue, or in dark green, or in any other homogenous colour.

This is a very important indication given to us by the appropriate use of colours.

I must remark that the sun disc, represented on these frescoes, was always coloured in red.

Thus the formation of the sign *YR* seems to indicate the union of the two essential principles of *RA*: the creating word and its visible manifestation the sun disc.

The word of God becoming flesh, according to St. John, reflects itself visibly in the physical organ of the eye. Or from another point of view, the man contemplates the result of his work and judges it by means of his reason.

Plato says concerning the eyes, that the gods created them before all other organs of the human body, in order to be " bearers of light," and they placed them in the head for the following motives : " They made that this portion of fire that has not got the faculty of burning, but the one of producing a mild light that never fails to enlighten us—became a physical body. It is like a pure and sensible fire which is placed in us. . . . When the daylight meets the current of the visual fire, then the similar is applied to its similar and joins so intimately one to another that they form one. According to the direction of the eyes the light coming from inside meets the one that arrives from the exterior objects." (Timeos.)

Thus the human eye presents a reflector of the

light, or to use the Egyptian terminology, the reflection of *Ra*, the sun. But at the same time it is also the organ by the means of which the reason of man contemplates and scrutinises the results of its work.

Therefore the ideographic representation of the word " to create, to make " by the means of the eye is logical, and conveys to our intelligence a deep philosophic meaning.

The god Ra was called " the Creator of the names of his members which were born in the forms of different gods."

The primitive gods, those that participated in the development of the Creation, were eight in number, forming with the god Ra, from whom they emanated, the number nine, called in the Egyptian teaching the " Great Ennead."

These eight gods descending from Ra can be considered as his faculties developed by the successive division of the Unity (I was one who became two, I was two who became four, I was four who became eight, but I am one who protects it).

I will return to this essential point of the Egyptian teaching later, and expound the development of the principle of Trinity into the form of pantheism generally accepted by the Egyptian religion. In the second part of this book I will explain the signification of the number nine according to the Hebraic Cabala. For the present I content myself with a rough sketch of this idea in its general lines to explain the meaning of the term " *ennead*."

In some texts the gods of this Ennead are called " the teeth and lips of the mouth (*Ra*) that proclaims the names of everything." In other texts Ra says :

" I have created all the forms with what came out of my mouth."

It is interesting to remark here that Moses, to express the action of the Creator, employed the word *BARA*, meaning " he created." The root from which derives this word is *Ra* (or *Re*). " It is the word *Re*," as says F. d'Olivet, " indicating the means by which one acts. This sign in the word ' *Bara* ' is combined with *B* which presents the assimilating principle," or in other words the reflection.

The homonymous sounds which constitute the name of the Egyptian god Ra and the root of the Hebraic word " to create " could possibly be regarded as due to coincidence, but one must not forget that Moses was an initiate of the Egyptian temples " who knew all the secrets," as is stated in the scriptures.

The so-called ancient Hebraic writing, that we study, dates only from the time of Hezdra and Daniel ; the primitive writing in which Moses had traced his books was lost during the captivity in Babylon. We have every reason to suppose that this primitive writing was borrowed by Moses from the Egyptians, and presented either the pure hieroglyphs or at least the so-called hieratic writing, which is a simplification of the hieroglyphs.

The employing of the word " *Re* " to express the idea of " means," or " tool," of the creation presents the exact rendering of the Egyptian teaching in which, as I have shown, the creating word *Ra* was considered as a tool, by the means of which the Creator accomplished the act of creation.

The fact that the Hebraic scriptures recognised " *Ra* " as the principal god of Egypt, is clearly stated in the Psalm lxxxvii, where Egypt is called "the country Ra-H-Ab," meaning: the country of which Ra is the father.

So *Ra* meant simultaneously the creating power, the verb (*logos*) and its visible manifestation—the sun, the source of existence on earth.

The god of speech, the one who, according to the ancient myth, taught the human beings the hiero-glyphic writing that fixed visibly the "words of God"—was the god *Thoth*. But we see also from the frescoes and we learn from the texts that *Thoth* was considered as being the moon god.

In his quality of god of speech *Thoth* is the delegate, the representative, of Ra-Logos, and in his role of moon god—*Thoth* is the reflection of the sun (*Ra*). Thus it is quite logical that in some texts *Thoth* is called "the lips," as it is the lips that combine in their movement the words emanated from the mouth, which is the organ characterising *Ra*. Therefore the ideographic representation of the lips naturally reminds us of the one that represents the moon. The difference, as you can see, is slight: the crescent of the moon has got exactly the same shape as the sign of the lip, only in the crescent one sees the centre of it reflecting the solar ray.

I recapitulate: God created the world by the means of His Word (*Ra*), which, being manifested, became the solar disc, and God contemplated the result of His deed through His eye (*YR*).

Man, created in the image of God, possesses the necessary elements for creating: the word and the faculty of seeing and judging the results of his work. But this last differs from the one accomplished by God, as man cannot create from nothing like his prototype, but only can transform the existing matter from one state to another.

The power of the word of man consists in the *naming* of beings or of things (" and whatsoever Adam called every living creature, that was the name thereof." Gen. ii, 19). This means that the name given to a manifestation by man constitutes the particular being of this precise form of life, or more distinctly—the relation between man and the being to which he gave a name.

The word " name " was written, as you remember, *RN*, representing ideographically the Logos fixed definitely in a state of stability, or in other words : " in the past " (as the sign *N* presents the one that defines the past and shows that a thing has no more movement in it, but is shaped definitely).

The correct composition of a name presents a sort of mathematical formula, which defines the named object or being. Thus the name being pronounced properly calls to life the being (or the object) that it defines. " Look at the tree," says a text, " its foliage appears when it is called by name."

But to be able to create by the power of the name one had to know and understand its composition.

This was called *Ma-Khrou*, meaning literally " to have the voice just," or in other terms, to understand the harmony of composition of the name which one pronounced. This expression did not mean knowledge of the grammatical composition of a name, but the understanding of the creating powers which entered in the formula of the precise being or object.

The sign *Ma* represents a flute and symbolises justice, harmony, rightfulness. Only one who understood the way to use this musical instrument could play a harmonious and pleasant melody; the one who did not know how to use it would only extract unmusical sounds forming a cacophony.

Thus one understands that the employing of the expression *Ma-Khrou* concerning a name meant that the one who pronounced it understood its composition and therefore could hope to obtain the necessary creative effect.

It is important to mention here the goddess of Justice, whose name was " Maat." This name was written by the hieroglyphics representing the sickle and the flute, and the female figure that determines this name wears on her headdress the ostrich feather, which is the symbol of " light."

The goddess Maat was the inseparable companion of Ra. She is called in the texts simultaneously " His mother, his daughter and his wife." Symbolically this means that the Creative Word (Logos) was born from the principle of justice—the Creator himself, and that every manifestation of the Logos is equally just and true.

This is also the reason why the title " *Ma-Khrou* " (" Just of voice ") applied to the deceased, made him one who deserved the great recompense of eternal life. A man " *Ma-Khrou* " became naturally the image of God Himself.

Another word which I have previously mentioned is *Per-Khrou*, meaning literally " the coming to life by the power of the voice." This word is closely attached to the preceding and constitutes its natural consequence and effect. The man who understood " the melody " of a name by pronouncing it in a correct voice or pronunciation (*Ma-Khrou*), could obtain the

PLATE IV

Yr. - the eye, to create, to see.

"He created the waters, He created the land" Pap Hunefer : Hymn to the Sun.

S - Mà - the sickle. S Mà - to look.

△ S 1 - Qmâ to fashion,
△ S 1 ... : "He fashions humanity" Pap Hunefer, : Hymn to the Sun.

- Mâ - the flute or the cubit
- the goddess Maat

Ma-Khrou - just of voice
Per-Khrou - the voice that animates

Shou - god of the air and of light, - the principle of expansion.

Tefnut, goddess of limitation
- "Father of Nut daughter of Ra" (Statue of Zed Hor).

Geb, god of the Earth.

Nut, goddess of the sky vault.

Osiris, god of fecondation.

11 ... or ... Isis - the mother earth.

12 ... Set, god of solid matter, (... the brick) and of involutive force (... Typhon).

13 ... Nephtys - the mistress of the temple

14 ... Sa, piece of cloth partly unrolled. God of human knowledge.

15 ... Mza - the book, sign determining an abstract idea.

16 ... Aton the sun disc

17 ... Hh - million of years.

18 ... Ntr. Mdw - "the words of God" (the hieroglyphic writing).

19 ... The god Nou the promatter.

20 ... Fn - to crawl and ... Fn - to breathe.

realisation in a precise form, of the named object or being (*Per-Khrou*).

We see these two words written on every funeral papyrus as well as on frescoes in tombs. The usual formula which accompanies the name and titles of the deceased states that " he is a *Ma-Khrou*," which one usually translates " justified."

As I have explained, a more correct rendering of the esoteric sense of this formula would be, that the deceased possesses the knowledge of the names of things, or in other words of their constructive organisation.

The offerings that are represented on the frescoes, as well as the scenes of life with its different pleasures, became realities for the deceased *Ma-Khrou*, as he made them come to life by the power of his creative voice, *Per-Khrou*.

The ancient science called " magic " is based upon these two essential principles : (1) the comprehension of the composition of the different combinations of natural forces and (2) the power to evoke to life (or destroy) these precise combinations by the sole use of the right word.

The Bible says : " I have killed them by the words of my mouth " (Hosea vi, 5), and elsewhere : " Is not my word as a fire ? and like a hammer that breaketh the rock in pieces ? " (Jer. xxiii, 29.)

The Egyptian incantation by which one paralysed the evil spirit, called the serpent *Apep*, begins by the words : " That his name would not exist. . . ."

An ancient legend says that when the god Ra was stung by a scorpion and was suffering agony, he called the great magician Isis, whom he asked to make the necessary incantations for the restoration of his health. Isis answered that, to be able to help him in his trouble she had to know his name. But Ra, knowing that the possession of his name would give Isis power over him, told her different names by which he was called, but not the real one. Her magic not being successful and the sufferings of the god becoming greater and greater, he at last decided to reveal his real name to Isis. Then she could at once restore his health, but received over him a dominating power.

The name, according to the Egyptian teaching, presents a part of the soul of a man—his individuality. We can understand from this point of view the care that the Egyptians took to preserve the name from destruction. And the prayers that we read in the Book of the Dead: " that my name would live for ever," " that my name would not stink," etc., become comprehensible and full of meaning.

When one wanted to punish a man or injure him, even after his death, one scratched his name written on a monument, or in the tomb, or even destroyed it altogether. We find very many examples of this kind of vengeance on Egyptian monuments, and the best known and most striking is the destruction of the name of Akhnaton—father-in-law of Tut-Ankh-Amon. This Pharaoh was the first who, long before Moses, had the idea of instituting monotheism. He replaced the adoration of all the ancient Egyptian gods of the pantheon by the one of the solar disc, *Aton*. The hymns that were found at Tel-Amarna, in which this god is glorified, are striking in their poetic and philosophic composition. The mistake of Akhnaton was, firstly, that the common Egyptian of his time was not yet ready to accept abstract ideas and could neither appreciate nor understand the new teaching. The second reason of his lack of success was that though the new school was trying to propagate deep and philosophic ideas concerning God and the Creation, the form in which it enveloped the idea of God was purely materialistic and known for ages as the physical solar disc.

Therefore one understands that the priests of the old school could not admit the vulgarisation of the great secret of the temples—the idea of the creative principle of Tem, especially so, as in the new teaching this principle was degraded to the role of a material manifestation—the sun disc. This is the reason why, after the death of the heretic Pharaoh, he was punished with the greatest of all punishments, the destruction of his name. His successor, who bore the name of Tut-Ankh-*Aton* (meaning "the living image of Aton"), changed it into Tut-Ankh-*Amon*, restoring thus his descent from the true god Amon, who was the particular form of the Creator according to the teaching of the Theban school.

I trust that I have conveyed a clear idea of the Egyptian doctrine concerning the creative power of the word manifested in the correct composition of the name.

CHAPTER IV

THE TRINITY DEVELOPING INTO PANTHEISM

THE reader remembers that, according to the Egyptian doctrine, the Reason of life, the One who emanated out of Himself all the infinite forms of the innumerable manifestations of Creation, was *Tem*, " the one of millions of years" (the " Ancient of Days," according to the Hebraic Cabala). The first act which started the Creation of the world was the division of the primordial principle into two (the father and the mother), expressed in the Egyptian texts by the formula *Mout-F* and in the Cabala by the " Balance that was in the Ancient of Days." This division constitutes the idea of a Trinity which was at the base of all of the ancient religions. The appearance of the two opposed principles : positive and negative, or masculine and feminine, or active and passive—necessitates the establishment of their mutual relation one towards the other. A being that has postulated " I " understands the difference between himself " I " and what is not himself, and at once establishes a relation between " I " and " not I." This relation presents the point of equilibrium between the two opposed principles. In the Hebraic Cabala this idea is expressed in the name composed of three letters, " *Iod*," presenting the active principle, " *He* "—the passive principle, and " *Vau* "—the one that simultaneously joins together the two opposed principles and separates them one from the other, not allowing either one of them to lose his particular individuality. Thus they are joined intimately together, but each of them presents nevertheless a particular and complete being, like the parents who unite to give birth to their child, who is simultaneously the descendant of the father and of the mother. But though the parents have united to give the possibility of a new life—they nevertheless stay separate and individual.

In the Hebraic Cabala the idea of the first trinity is given by the three Sephiroths: "*Kether*"—the crown, the reason; "*Chochma*"—"*cognitio,*" knowledge, the understanding; and "*Binah*"—"*ratio,*" the reasonable principle, presenting the deductions made by the man out of his comprehension.

The Alexandrian school expressed the same idea (which it attributed to Hermes Trismegistos) in the following terms: "The Father is the idea, the Son —the word, and their union presents the third principle which is Life."

The Christian Trinity is composed, as you know, of the Father (Reason), the Son (Logos), and the Holy Ghost; the respective roles of whom are very similar to those expressed by the Alexandrian school.

In many pagan religions the basic trinity is comprised in the form of a divine family composed of the father, the mother, and the child; for example, in Egypt there were Osiris, Isis, and their son Horus. This basic principle of the primitive division—Trinity, is developed in the Egyptian religion in the so-called Ennead, or nine principal gods of the Pantheon.

The same idea is expounded in the book of Genesis by the opposing of one element to another: the light and the darkness, the waters above (sky) and the waters below (sea), the waters (humidity) and the earth (dryness), etc. . . .

In the Hebraic Cabala the idea of the Egyptian Ennead finds an echo in the so-called Sephirothic system which presents the attributes of God in his different manifestations through the infinite forms of Creation.

The Egyptian Ennead, according to the teaching of the ancient school of Heliopolis, was developed as follows :

The first act of the Creator *Tem* was the emanation of his word *Ra* (Logos). But this first-born son of god was simultaneously the principle of life and of light, an idea that was expressed in the Egyptian doctrine by the fact that the name *Ra* meant simultaneously "the word in action" and "the sun"— centre of light and reason of life on earth.

Thus *One* became *Two*, or according to the Egyptian ideographic writing : *Tem*—the Reason, the sole possibility of life, who was *Mout-F* (or according to the Hebraic Cabala, had the Balance in himself, meaning that the principle of division was in potential in the unity of god), *Tem* became *Tem-Ra :* the reason joined to the manifestation, " the lamp and the flame."

As I have shown, we find this combined name in the oldest texts that we possess : those of the Pyramids.

Following the announced principle of division, *Ra* manifested the Creation by consecutive divisions of his proper essence. This division was accomplished by the emanation of four couples formed each of a masculine and a feminine principle—a husband and a wife, or, in other terms, a positive and a negative force. The consecutiveness of these divisions presents the logical development of a manifestation beginning by the establishment of the principle which is gradually defined, passing from an abstract idea to a concrete effect.

The first couple emanated from *Ra* were *Shou* and *Tefnut*.

Shou personified the principle of *light* and at the same time the principle of *air*—the two elements which are indispensable for all the manifestations of life. Thus one can say that *Shou* presents the essence of possibility of life. Abstractly, this god expressed the principle of expansion, or of evolution. This expansion would naturally be infinite if its propagation would not be opposed by the principle of limitation, which was personified by the goddess *Tef-Nut*.

We read in a text concerning the Creation of the first couple: " Ra breathed and the god Shou appeared, then Ra created (fashioned) the goddess Tefnut " (papyrus Nu. Ch., 130, 4).

The book of Genesis expresses this phase of creation by the apparition of light which in the Hebraic text was rendered literally : " Something distended and rarefied." To the light the Bible opposes the darkness called " the compressing and hardening power" which is rendered by the Hebraic word *TEW*. In the phonetic of this last word we can easily trace the Egyptian name *TEF-NUT*.

As I said, the couples emanating progressively from Ra are composed each of a masculine active principle, personified by a god, and a feminine passive principle, personified by a goddess. Thus in the first couple the masculine principle will be *Shou* and the feminine *Tefnut*. But the words "masculine" and "feminine" must not be understood in the common and literal sense. We must not regard these two divinities as being absolutely and only persons of opposite sex. This is correct only in regard to their mutual relations. What we call "masculine" will be the active principle, and what we call "feminine" will be the passive principle, the one that creates an opposition to the expansion of the action of the first.

Thus, in the first couple, *Tefnut* will be the feminine or passive part in regard to *Shou*, but in regard to the following manifestations of opposing powers, *Tefnut* will be the principle, and according to the Egyptian teaching will be therefore considered as masculine.

You will understand from this point of view the statement which we find in the Egyptian teaching that calls *Tefnut* simultaneously, "daughter of Ra and father of Nout," inscription on the statue of Zed Hor.

Nout is the name of the goddess of the sky belonging to the second couple emanated from *Ra*. Thus *Nout* personifies the manifested boundary of expansion of the air, the vault of the sky, and presents therefore the realisation of the principle of limitation announced in *Tefnut*. This is the reason why *Tefnut*, according to the idea of the Egyptian teaching, was qualified as being the *father* (principle) of *Nout—Tef-Nut* (*Tef*, father).

The whole following system of consecutive division is developed on two lines opposed one to the other. The principle of expansion, or of evolution, expressed by the god *Shou*; and the principle of limitation, or hardening, or in other terms the involutive force.

F

This second line is developed out of the principle personified by *Tefnut*.

The second couple emanated from *Ra* were *Geb*, the earth, and *Nut*, the vault of the sky.

These two divinities present the precision of the principle of limitation announced by *Tefnut*, as they are the natural limits between which develop all the manifestations of life. Symbolically, these limits

Fig. 4.

The gods Geb and Nut separated by Shou. Tamoni papyrus.

express the concept that the activity of man evolves between elevation towards the sky representing his spirituality, and the attraction of the earth which constitutes his material part.

We can observe very interesting representations of these divinities on numerous frescoes and on papyri which show ideographically the idea that I have expounded. *Geb* is represented lying on the ground and *Nout* as bending over him, forming by the shape of her body a suggestive image of the sky vault.

Shou is kneeling between them in the effort to separate their union with his uplifted arms. The idea that the artist wanted to convey by this picture represents exactly the effort of the principle of expansion to burst the material limitations opposed to its propagation.

I have said concerning *Nut* that her principle, or

Fig. 5.

The god Geb.

according to the Egyptian definition—her " father," was *Tefnut*.

Geb (or *Seb*) is called in the texts simultaneously : the " son and the father," as he is the son of God and the father of man—the link that unites the human inhabitants of the earth to the Primitive Reason of Creation. The denomination " son " is clearly expressed by the use of the appropriate sign of the goose, which, as you know, expresses the descent " son of so-and-so."

Pursuing his division, Ra emanated simultaneously two couples : *Osiris-Isis* and *Seth-Nephthys*. Regarded as a whole, each of these couples is opposed one to the other, presenting, one (Osiris-Isis)—the development of the *principle of expansion* personified by *Shou*, and the other (Seth-Nephthys)—the personification of the *principle of limitation* of *Tefnut*. But apart from that each couple judged by itself presents the idea of the principle (or active force), and the one of opposition (the passive counter-action) personified respectively by the masculine and feminine personalities forming each couple.

The first couple (Osiris-Isis) presents in its whole the power of fecundation, or the *evolutive power* of life which manifests itself on earth in the grain as well as in every animal form and in man.

Isis was the one that conceived, the mother. Metaphorically, *Osiris* was often individualised as the grain and *Isis* as the earth in which the grain had to be buried to germinate ; or, as the Egyptians said : " joined itself to the earth " to give the possibility of the mystery of life to be manifested. Other allegorical texts personified *Osiris* as the Water and *Isis* as the Mud of the Nile, which, being joined to the water, gives life to the innumerable beings in the valley.

The name of Osiris was written *Ast-Re*, and the name of Isis *Ast*. As you can see, both these names are formed by the sign of the throne *Ast*, but in the name of Isis *the seat is unoccupied*, and in the name of Osiris we see the sign of the eye, *Yr*, the creating power which has taken its seat on the throne.

In other texts, instead of the eye we see in the name of Osiris the sign of the sun occupying the throne, thus this name can be interpreted literally " the throne of Ra," indicating the means by which the creative power of the Logos manifests itself in life. As you will observe, both these representations express the same idea.

For the name of *Isis* we find in some texts (for example on the sarcophagus of Panechem-Ast) an expression which phonetically is the same as the throne and symbolically means " the sacred land of burial," alluding to the grain that needs to be buried in order to spring up in a new form of life.

The creation of this couple corresponds in the Bible to the following sentence : " And God said : let the earth bring forth grass, the herb yielding seed and the fruit tree yielding fruit after his kind whose seed is in itself upon the earth. . . . And the earth brought grass. . . ." (Gen. i, 11, 12.)

In this passage of the book of Genesis we see the same idea of the union of the fecundating principle with the earth (the mother that conceives and brings forth the manifestation of new life).

In many Egyptian tombs one has found the so-called " germinating Osiris " which presents a sheet of linen stretched on a wooden frame on which grains were sown, following the outline of the body of Osiris. They were afterwards well watered until green grass had grown about a couple of inches high. The belief thus depicted was that the germinating power of Osiris would effect the restoration of life to the buried body, as it had done to the grain on the image of Osiris. This proceeding constituted part of the funeral ritual presenting the so-called imitative or sympathetic magic.

The last couple emanated from Ra, and which in its whole is opposed to the previous one, is formed also of two divinities: the masculine principle *Seth*, and the feminine manifestation *Nephthys*. This couple is the definite manifestation of the principle of limitation, a development of *Tefnut*, therefore, it presents the hardening, the dryness and abstractly the force of involution.

The name of *Seth* was written determined by the image of an animal called by the Greeks " typhonic," which it is difficult to define by its representation. The sign that delineates the formation of the name *Seth* represents a brick. Thus the name of this god gives the idea of a material construction, or more precisely of its principle—the brick. It is interesting to follow the meaning given to the name of *Seth* in different religious doctrines developed out of the Egyptian teaching. As you see in the latter, the god *Seth* is simultaneously defined by the typhonic animal (a personification of evil) and the brick—the principle of construction, its foundation.

The book of Genesis (iv, 24) says that Eve " bore a son and called his name Seth: for God, said she, hath appointed me another seed instead of Abel. . . ."

Now the name *Seth*, or *Sheth*, according to the Hebraic writing, means " the base," the foundation, and the Hebrew commentators represented him as the father of the model family, *the base* on which was built all the progeny of the chosen nation.

The Arabs, on the contrary, form of the same root the name Shaith-an, the devil, an idea which, as I have shown, was also conserved in the Greek rendering of the name, Typhon, the evil spirit.

Thus we see clearly how both the ideas of the Egyptian god *Seth*, that were simultaneously represented in the hieroglyphic name, were separated and interpreted differently in the teachings of different nations which inherited their principles from the same source.

If one identifies oneself with the ancient Egyptian in accepting this point of view, one can understand how these two apparently opposed ideas could be combined in one divine personality.

For the ancient Egyptian *Seth* was not the principle of darkness, nor the personification of evil that we would call the " devil." From the point of view of the evolutive power which was developed in the couple, *Osiris-Isis—Seth* was the *opposing power*, the force of involution, or in other words the materialisation of an idea. You remember that the principle from which evolved the couple *Osiris-Isis*, was *Shou*, that of expansion. The principle that manifested itself definitely in *Seth* was that of limitation enounced by *Tefnut*. Even as the evolutive force is indispensable for the conception and birth of a being—the involutive force is necessary to render possible the material realisation of this being. In man we see the constant struggle between these two currents : the one trying to elevate his spirituality and the other maintaining him in the boundaries of his body. Each of these courses is indispensable to the incarnated life and likewise it is indispensable to the life of all the Universe. Without the evolutive current man would become inanimate, he would congeal to the state of a stone, but without the involutive current he would become disincarnated, cease to be a man, becoming only a spiritual being.

One can judge of the importance which the Egyptians attributed to *Seth* from the role this god played in the funeral ritual, where he is one of the four gods who act to restore the rigidity of the body of the deceased.

Some texts attribute to *Seth* the restoration of the backbone, the foundation of the body. But from other texts we learn that it was *Osiris* who was considered the ruler of the spine. How are we to reconcile these seeming contradictions? It is quite simple and logical: both these gods spread their influence on the back of the man. *Osiris* gave it the magnetic power, " the fluidic force coming from the back " according to the Egyptian terminology.

We can see, therefore, that the influence of Osiris reigns over the nervous centres that are in the spine, the so-called " grey matter," the role of which in the life of man is known to our science.

Seth on the contrary governs the solid part of the back, the back-bone, giving rigidity to the whole body and making it keep upright. Thus the two opposed principles find the possibility of living together in the same part of the human body, and each plays an important and definite role.

The same thing can be said about the relations of the two opposed gods in the macrocosmos. Each of them is indispensable, and without either of them life in the material world would be impossible. But for the manifestation of life these two principles must be in constant struggle, as it is precisely this continual fight which conditions incarnated life. I will come back to this question in the chapter concerning the Sephiroths and will expound the way in which this idea was expressed by the Hebraic Cabala, which is very much the same as its Egyptian prototype.

In the teachings evolved out of the Egyptian religion each concerned itself with only one part of the idea expressed by the name of the god *Seth*.

The Hebrews dwelt upon the constructive side of *Seth* and based upon this foundation the development of the whole of their nation. The Greeks and the Arabs saw on the contrary only the apparently dark part of this god and for them he became a personification of evil.

The wife of *Seth* was the goddess *Nephthys*, whose name can be interpreted " the mistress of the temple." In the name of this goddess we see clearly the dominating idea of the Egyptian teaching which was based on the belief in the final victory of the evolutive power, which must inevitably bring all creation back to its principle.

You remember that in a divine couple the masculine part presents the principle and the feminine part the realisation of it. Thus the principle enounced by the name of *Seth* was *the brick*, the constructive power of nature. In its realisation—*Nephthys*—we see that this power is not orientated towards the construction of a palace or of a fortress, but to the building of the *temple* in which man will adore God.

I think that this point alone is sufficient to illustrate the greatness and deep spirituality of the Egyptian teaching.

In the legend of Osiris, which presents the constant fight between the two creative powers of nature, as well as the idea of the eternal resurrection of life— Osiris was killed and cut in pieces by *Seth*, but his body was found and restored to wholeness by the hands of *Isis* and *Nephthys*. Thus we see the two opposed forces (the one of evolution and the one of involution) working together for the restoration of the generating principle.

To the Great Ennead is added a tenth principle which is in exact correspondence with the Hebraic "tree of Sephiroths," composed of ten elements. This tenth element is the synthesis of all the preceding elements, as the last Sephiroth "Malcuth" synthesises the previous attributes of God.

In the Egyptian teaching this synthetic principle is personified in the god *Horus*, "the son of Isis," otherwise called "the avenger of his father." One must not confuse this god with the ancient solar divinity—the hawk "*Hor*."

The Greeks called *Horus* the son of Isis—"Harpocratos," or "Horus the child." He is represented in the form of a child, with the typical lock of hair, and holding one finger to his mouth.

According to the legend, *Horus* the child fought and conquered the murderer of his father. He was appointed by the Creator as the sole ruler of Egypt, and was the first to join "the two lands."

Thus we see in this legend the confirmation of the dominating idea of the Egyptian teaching which I have explained already—the definite victory of the forces of good over those of evil.

The Egyptian pantheon contains many other divinities forming secondary Enneads which are all composed after the model of the Great Ennead that I have analysed. Most of these divinities present personifications of different natural forces which acted in the creation of the world and particularly of man.

It would take too long to explain all their particular roles, and I think that the analysis of the Great Ennead gives a sufficient idea of the principles of the Egyptian religion.

There is one point to which I want to draw your particular attention—it is the cult of Osiris in the Egyptian religion. As you remember, the primitive cult was essentially solar. Man saw in the daily apparition of the sun's disc the life that is constantly resuscitated from death. With time was instituted the cult of Osiris that gradually spread over all Egypt and became its principal religion. In regard to man, Osiris was the prototype of a perfect and sinless being, who sacrificed his life—died, and was justified by the court of judges of the Other World. Though Osiris became the mummy-god, the king of the dead—he was eternally resuscitating, giving the example to man of the resurrection which every justified deceased received as a recompense for his good life on earth. Thus the Pharaoh and later every deceased Egyptian received the name of Osiris, as he orientated his life so as to be justified after death and obtain the recompense in the image of this god. Therefore the introduction of the Osirian cult gave birth in Egypt to the moral, which prevails over the magic teaching of the ancient religion.

Formerly it was considered that the knowledge of the names of gods of the underworld opened infallibly the gates to the deceased. After the general spreading of the cult of Osiris, it became necessary to live a " just life " on earth which gave the certitude of obtaining the beatitude and the resurrection as recompense.

We see this in numerous moral treaties like, for

example, the so-called " Instructions of Ptah-Hotep to his son," or " the Admonition of Prince Merikhara," which approach very closely to the teaching of Christian moral. And we can say with Merejkovsky that Osiris was " the shadow of the Crucified," both in their death and in their resurrection, instituting the necessity of a pure and moral life in order to obtain resurrection and eternal life.

CHAPTER V

SYNTHESIS

I HOPE that I have made it clear that the ancient thought, which created the doctrine of the Egyptian initiatory schools, shines brightly through the apparent enigmas of the conventional symbolism and the metaphoric images, under which the initiates hid their dominant ideas.

This brief exposition was necessary for the understanding of what follows, and will enable us to penetrate into the secrets of the so-called occult sciences.

To do this we must pursue our research into the Hebraic doctrine which followed immediately the Egyptian teaching and which presents the next link of the same chain of the ancient tradition.

I have often had to refer to the Hebraic scriptures in order to throw light on the enigmas of the Egyptian doctrine. In studying the Hebraic Cabala I shall follow the same method and refer to the Egyptian teaching in order to show the source from which the Hebraic civilisation borrowed its ideas. Thus the difficulties of some of the Cabalistic systems will be cleared away.

As it has been observed, the Egyptian teaching is not the earliest knowledge received by man from the first revelation. We have no means of determining the first religion of the earth, neither the first language, which evidently possessed the creative power of the Logos. The study of the origin of different languages, not having apparently any connection with one another, and used by nations which lived very far apart from one another, nevertheless reveals some points possessed in common which prove that all were developed from one common root.

The Egyptian hieroglyphic writing in its ideographic signification affords the best example and the easiest means of understanding the formation of the primitive idea. This is the reason why I have taken for basis that particular writing and have put before you on general lines the principles of the religious doctrine and the philosophic thought of that civilisation. Other ancient languages, as for example the Chinese or the Sanscrit, by the stylisation of the primitive hieroglyphic, make it much more difficult for us to trace the idea to its origin—its graphic representation. But nevertheless, a careful and attentive study allows us to reconstruct the primitive glyph, and we are struck by the fact that in all these languages the generating thought was apparently the same.

The monuments of art brought to light by the excavations of the last fifty years present in their composition and especially in their ornament the best and undoubted proof of the common origin of the basic ideas interpreted in different civilisations by the same ideographic sign, which had only evolved differently according to the particular individuality of a nation.

In the last part of my present book I will give some examples of this interpretation from which can be clearly seen the evolution of the same idea in a particular civilisation.

To return to Egypt. As I have shown, Egypt cannot be considered the cradle of the primitive thought, nor as the country in which were born the principles of religion. I have stated in the introduction that what we call Egyptian civilisation was imported from outside in full blossom by conquerors who colonised the Nile valley some 5000 years before our era. It took some centuries for that imported civilisation to be adopted by the primitive inhabitants of Egypt and to take root in the conception of the ancient Egyptian as his own belief, the creed that he inherited from his ancestors and through them from the gods.

Now naturally one asks oneself the question : from whence came these conquerors, and who were the men who possessed at such a remote time such a wonderful philosophic conception, as well as such a high standard, of art and science ?

Many scholars have proposed different hypotheses to answer these questions. All these hypotheses can be classified under three different heads.

First.—Some consider the conquerors of Egypt as being of Semitic origin and having come from the East, from Asia. They base this hypothesis on the fact that in the Egyptian language there exists a certain number of roots which apparently are Semitic. Another point on which this theory is based is the knowledge of the use of burned bricks, which was imported into Egypt by the conquerors and which was also known in Assyria.

But to this one can answer, that Egypt, becoming a world kingdom which encircled in its boundaries the whole of the known world extending to the frontiers of India—entered necessarily into relations with the Semitic inhabitants of the conquered countries, and borrowed from them some of their knowledge, as also some foreign words and expressions were introduced into the Egyptian language.

We see by the study of contemporary languages how, in the course of time, by contact between different nations, words belonging to a foreign tongue, which either strike the imagination by their queerness, or seem to express an idea better than the word of one's own tongue—take root in a language and gradually come to be regarded as belonging to that language.

It is unnecessary to give examples here, as I think that this is self-evident. Especially in English it is easy to trace a word either to its Latin, or German, or Gallic origin.

I will give here only one very simple example taken from the French, to show how a word belonging to a foreign tongue becomes in course of time, with a slight adaptation, one which is considered of pure French origin. We know that the first to invent the pocket-knife were the English. Pocket-knives were later exported from England to other countries, and first of all, naturally, to France. The English word " knife " became in the French pronunciation " *canif*," as the Frenchmen, seeing this word written, thought it necessary to pronounce the sound *K* dropped in the English pronunciation, and accompanied it by a vowel, as is characteristic in the French language.

This example gives an idea of the adaptation of a foreign word into a language, with the result that the borrowed word appears indigenous to the language that had borrowed it.

The same thing probably happened in Ancient Egypt, as the words which seem to us of Semitic origin appear later in the language, but are not employed in the first texts known to us.

Another fact that might seem insignificant has, in my opinion, the greatest importance and proves the mistake of the theory which derives Egyptian civilisation from the East. As we know, the Camel, which was such an important factor in the life of Egypt since the time of the Arab conquest, and which to the present day is still the principal means of communication in the desert, was imported from Asia, which is the birthplace of this species of animal.

If the Pharaonic inhabitants had arrived from Asia they would have certainly brought with them this animal that was domesticated there a long time ago, and had become the sole and most important means of transport. But in ancient Egyptian texts we see nothing of the sort. There does not even exist a hieroglyphic representing a camel, though we find elephants, giraffes, and all kinds of antelopes and other animals characteristic of the fauna of Africa.

On some frescoes of the New Kingdom, in scenes depicting relations with foreigners of Semitic race, one sees the representation of the camel as being characteristic of the identification of the race that used it. The same applies to the horse, which appears in Egypt only in the time of the XVIIIth dynasty, and which long before that time was known and employed by Semites of ancient Asia. I will not stop to discuss other points which prove to us that the origin of Egyptian civilisation cannot be traced to Asia.

The second hypothesis, which considers the conquerors of the tribes of the Nile valley as having come from the south, is based principally upon the fact that the Egyptian religion possesses certain characteristics which are common to races inhabiting Central Africa. In particular we can observe that the Pharaonic Egyptians believed in the existence of a fabulous country called " Punt " which was somewhere in the south towards the sources of the Nile, and which was considered the place of birth of the gods and first men.

It is obvious that some of the ancient rites were common to different tribes, or nations which were dispersed on the continent of Africa. In introducing their own deeply philosophic teaching, the conquerors of Egypt did not abolish some of the ancient customs, but acted very gently so as not to shock the beliefs of the conquered people. They introduced some of the primitive divinities into their pantheon and sanctified the rites which were performed for ages in the Nile valley. By acting in this way they were sure to conquer the souls of the primitive people who believed that the new religion was the one of their ancestors and therefore accepted it without any opposition.

The fabulous country of Punt was, as I said, supposed to be at the sources of the Nile. Thus it was naturally considered as the birthplace of the vivifying power which in Egypt was personified by the Nile. Later on, when Egypt became a great kingdom and was renowned for its power and riches, expeditions were sent to explore this fabulous country, and brought back with them gold, precious stones, and precious incense which was extracted from trees grown in these southern parts, as well as the trees themselves, and animals unknown in Egypt, and also dwarfs belonging to certain tribes of Central Africa. We see on frescoes of the funerary temple of Queen Hatshepsut the representation of the arrival of one of these expeditions, and in the courtyard of the above-mentioned temple, now completely excavated, we can trace remains of roots of the trees which we observe in the frescocs, brought and planted.

Very interesting details have thus been brought to light concerning the relations of Egypt with other nations, as well as the formation of the Egyptian religion, but this is quite insufficient to prove the origin of the conquerors of prehistoric times.

There remains the last hypothesis, that the conquest was made from the *north*.

This seems to be well based upon the legend of the ancient teaching, which considers the Delta as the birthplace of Horus " the son of Osiris." In one of the most ancient known texts representing this legend in a form of a mystery, or play, we see that Horus, " the heir of the North land," became, after the struggle with his enemy, Seth, the first to join " the two lands," the north as well as the south (the last was previously under the rule of Seth).

The army that made the conquest was called " the followers of Horus," and this nomenclature persists in the funeral ritual to the end. The priests who performed this ritual were called " followers of Horus," and wore a characteristic band on their shoulder. Their role consisted in fighting the evil powers and in restoring life to the deceased as it was restored to the murdered Osiris by his son Horus, called the " Avenger of his father."

Apart from this very important statement of the ancient texts, we see on some old frescoes the representation of ships on which arrived the " followers of Horus," and these ships are shown very clearly as not being of the kind of boat commonly used on the

Nile, but as having high sides and showing by their special outline qualities necessary for *sea-going vessels*.

Thus it seems obvious that the conquerors who colonised Egypt and imported their very highly developed civilisation *came by sea from north*. But this does not solve our problem, nor does it furnish the possibility of establishing their country of origin. We shall have to turn here to legends and traditions of folklore and myths of other civilisations.

The excavations of the present century have removed the veil from many ancient mysteries and have given us proofs of the fact that underlying the origin of a myth there is always an historic fact. The poetic description by Homer of the mythical battle of Troy, the palace and labyrinth of King Mynos; the towns mentioned in the Biblical texts—all these accounts which, up to the end of last century, were considered as myths due to the poetic imagination of ancient peoples—became in our days uncontested historic realities.

It is necessary, therefore, to study with the greatest care the documents that we possess and not consider them, *a priori*, as only the result of pure imagination. This study, checked by documents of different civilisations, might give us an idea of the origin of the unique civilisation and explain many things which without it are incomprehensible. The further development of our material resources will perhaps allow us one day to excavate concrete proofs of facts which for the present we can only establish by logical deduction.

In the dialogue known as the *Timeos*, Plato makes Solon put questions to an Egyptian hierophant who informs him that the origin of the Egyptian civilisation was the lost continent of Atlantis. The Egyptian priest gives to Solon some details concerning the early history of Atlantis and outlines the plan of the town and sanctuary of the sun which constituted the centre from which emanated knowledge and religion. Further details of the story of Atlantis as told to Solon by the priests of Sais are furnished by Plato in the dialogue known as the *Critias*.

A fragment from a lost work of Theopompus of Chios, an historian of the fourth century B.C., speaks of a country lying in the Atlantic Ocean which he calls " Meropian," the inhabitants of which had attained a great height of civilisation and power. He states the fact of their conquest of Europe and the introduction of their culture on the shores of the Mediterranean.

We find a similar statement in the works of Proclus, who says that the inhabitants of islands in the Atlantic Ocean preserved the memory of a much larger island called Atlantis, which spread its dominion far away from the metropolis.

Strabo says that the account of Plato ought not to be regarded as fiction, and that such a continent as Atlantis might well have existed and disappeared.

From another point of view the evidence of Central American archæology seems to confirm the idea that at some remote time there existed in the Atlantic Ocean a common centre of civilisation which spread to the west as well as to the east, and that the Egyptian, Cretan, and Phœnician civilisations were its ramifications as well as those of the first conquerors of America, " which came by sea from the East." The monuments (pyramids, solar temples, and burials), as well as the religious teaching and writing of the

American " Maya " civilisation, seem to have striking points of resemblance with those that we find in Egypt and Crete.

It would take too long to give all the existing proofs confirming this postulate. I will content myself with saying that the prototype of the Egyptian and American pyramids is obviously the fabulous " Aztlan," the primitive hill which first appeared from the waters at the day of creation. According to Plato's description,

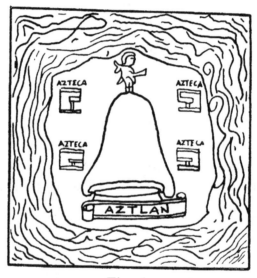

Fig. 6.

Aztlan—the primordial hill.

in the centre of the town of Atlantis there was a great pyramid, on the top of which was the temple consecrated to the sun.

The report of Cortez and the plan attached to it by him shows the ancient town of Mexico which seems to correspond exactly to the description of the town of Atlantis given by Plato ; *and in the centre of it we see the great pyramid surrounded on four sides by water.*

This does not mean that ancient Mexico was actually the town of Atlantis, but only that it was built on the model of the metropolis by the colonisers who arrived from the submerged continent.

We find a striking fact in Egypt that confirms the origin of the pyramid as being the same as that of the ancient American religion. According to the writings of Greeks who visited Egypt at the decline of its civilisation, some hundred of years B.C., the pyramids of Giza were surrounded by a canal and one could go round them in boats. Up to last year this was considered as a fiction and as one of the legends that are not based on real facts. But the latest excavations near the temple of the Sphinx brought to light two granite piers which descend into a canal and bear traces of boats which were tied up to them.

In this piece of canal now excavated *there still is water*, though the level of it is much higher than the one of the Nile. Apparently there exists a water-proof layer that does not allow the water to get away. It is quite probable that further excavations will bring to light the continuation of the canal, and then the Greek legend will become a fact.

In the so-called Cenotaph of Seti I in Abydos we see the mythical *hill* on which was established the symbolic burial place of the Pharaoh surrounded on all sides by a canal over twenty feet deep, fed by underground springs.

Lastly, in Dahshour a pyramid of an unidentified king was lately excavated, and it is surrounded on four sides by a sinusoidal brick wall built with the greatest care and representing exactly the hieroglyphic sign of water. Probably in this district the rock did not allow them to dig deep enough to obtain real water, so it was indicated by its symbol. This kind of symbolism in the Egyptian architecture was very common, and I will give some examples of it when I speak of the symbolism of art.

To all that has been said I must add that the word pyramid means " the coming out to birth," symbolising the first appearance of a precise formation (the mythic hill Aztlan) from the pro-matter—the Nou, or in other words, from the waters which were considered as being the mother of elements. And the Egyptian texts state that everything " is born from the Nou (or from the primitive mass of waters)," and elsewhere that " the deceased returns into the Nou."

Thus it was obvious from the point of view of the ancient Egyptian that the burial place, which is simultaneously the cradle of new life, would be the pyramid, which by its idea represents birth, and that this pyramid should be surrounded by water symbolising the pro-matter.

I cannot dwell on details and can only outline the facts that seem to convey to our intelligence that the place from which was imported the so-called Egyptian civilisation was the fabled Atlantis, which left in the memory of different people and of civilisations separated one from another by thousands of miles the idea of the birthplace of primitive knowledge and power.

All the researches made in the last fifty years in certain regions of the Atlantic Ocean by scientific expeditions seem to confirm the possibility of the existence in a remote age of a continent that disappeared under the water. These testimonies have been recorded elsewhere.

Thus I think that we can establish the role of Egypt as being *the link* that connects our western civilisations and religions with the old prehistoric teaching which perhaps was the primitive source of all the different ramifications of the ancient knowledge on earth. I say perhaps, because we do not possess any definite proofs and for the present cannot affirm that Atlantis was actually the cradle of human knowledge. Perhaps on the contrary it was also only one of the links of the primitive tradition, the one that preceded the Egyptian culture.

The Hebraic teaching which we are going to study in the following chapter presents the next link in the same chain, and is closely connected with the Egyptian teaching. This is the reason why, in the study of the Hebraic doctrine and Cabala, I shall often have recourse to the Egyptian teaching in order to throw light on what might otherwise seem obscure and arbitrary.

I repeat that Egypt must be considered as the oldest known link of the universal chain of the tradition and that its thought presents the base on which are founded all the posterior religions and philosophic systems.

Strabo states that during his visit to Egypt about the year 20 B.C., he was shown the rooms in the Heliopolis school that were occupied by Plato for thirteen years when he studied the Egyptian knowledge.

The Bible gives us testimony that Moses was also an initiate of the Egyptian temples, and the Hebraic scriptures are very often a literal translation of the Egyptian texts. I have shown that the book of Genesis and the Gospel of St. John borrowed their basic idea concerning the creative power of the Word from the teaching of the hierophants. One short example will be sufficient to show to what a point some of the biblical scriptures were an exact reproduction of the books that expounded the teaching of the Egyptians.

The words of the " Wise King " (Solomon) in the Hebrew book of Proverbs and the " Book of Wisdom " called the " Admonitions of Amenemope " begin as follows :

Amenemope.

Incline thine ear and hear my sayings,

And apply thine heart to their comprehension.

For it is a profitable thing to put them in thy heart,

But woe to him who transgresses them.

iii, 9–12.

Remove not the land mark on the boundary of the fields.

.   .   .   .

Be not greedy for a cubit of land,

And trespass not on the boundary of the widow.

vii, 12–15.

Proverbs.

Incline thine ear and hear words of the wise,

And apply thine heart unto my knowledge.

For it is a pleasant thing if thou keep them within thee,

If they be established together upon thy lips.

xxii, 17–18.

Remove not the ancient land mark,

And enter not into the fields of the fatherless.

xxiii, 10.

I could extend these examples *ad infinitum*, but I think that this short fragment is sufficient to give you an idea to what extent the Hebraic scriptures reproduced the Egyptian books of knowledge, either in literal translation or in any case in paraphrase.

In conclusion, I will only point out the two principal lines along which the Egyptian teaching developed.

The first was the knowledge, and the application of it which was given by magic power. This part was respectively under the domination of the gods *Sa* and *Heka*. The name of the first was written by the sign *Sa*, representing ideographically a piece of cloth partly unrolled. This shows metaphorically the knowledge that "unrolls itself" gradually in the intelligence of man.

The name *Heka* was determined by the sign of the hind-quarters of an animal, which, as you know, symbolised power. On frescoes in many tombs of the Valley of Kings at Luxor, on which is represented the "Book of what is in the Other World," we see the sun-boat traversing the shadowy channels of Hades. In the bows of the boat stands the god *Sa*, and in the stern, manipulating the paddles, one sees the god *Heka*. This expresses the idea, that *it is knowledge that opens the path* for the reasonable being, but that it is the *magic power that directs his acts* and makes him advance on the chosen path.

The second direction to which is orientated the Egyptian teaching is moral, the belief of a recompense for the just and the punishment for the unjust. The prototype of this second branch is given in the legend of Osiris, and this teaching provided a base for biblical as well as for Christian morality.

I hope that I have made it clear what part ancient Egypt has played in the formation of our conceptions as well as of our philosophic schools, and of the teachings of different religions.

PART II

THE HEBRAIC CABALA

CHAPTER I

PRINCIPLES OF THE LANGUAGE

IN the first part of this book we have studied the hieroglyphic language, and I have shown to you how the primitive idea found expression in the direct representation of an object. This constitutes the so-called ideographic meaning, the one that did not necessitate any learning on a man's part, nor even a knowledge of how to read or write. He traced as well as he could the image of what he saw, and thus conveyed the idea of his visual impression to his fellow-men. I have shown how, in the course of time, the ideographic writing transformed itself into symbolic and yet later into phonetic expression of abstract ideas. This evolution followed the development of thought in man, representing his growth from the state of childhood to that of a reasonable being, capable of analysing impressions received from outside and of making deductions applicable to his own individuality. The study of the Egyptian hieroglyphic writing is therefore necessary and important, as it gives us an opportunity of following the gradual formation of a tongue. As I have said, the hieroglyphics are the only ancient language in which the primitive ideographic image was preserved intact and combined itself naturally and intimately with the phonetic or alphabetic writing. In all other languages that we know, the evolution took place a long time ago and the signs which we see present either the stylisation of the primitive glyph (as is found, for example, in Chinese), or the ideographic sign was dropped altogether and the writing was reduced to a certain number of purely conventional letters expressing the phonetic sound, as is the case in all contemporary languages. Thus the language, becoming exclusively phonetic, long ago lost all trace of the primitive representation of the object.

The Hebraic writing belongs to the second group, presenting one of the phonetic languages, but at the same time it possesses some peculiarities in which it differs from other exclusively phonetic writings, and which allow for the co-existence in the same word (expressed by a number of signs) of different meanings. These meanings do not contradict, but on the contrary complete one another, affording a deeper penetration into the essence of the thought which they unveil more or less according to the stage of evolution at which the student has arrived.

As I have said, the first writing used by Moses was probably hieroglyphic or hieratic. This seems quite natural, as the creator of the Hebraic religion was an initiate of Egyptian temples and, according to the statement of the Bible, possessed the perfect knowledge of the secrets of the " divine tongue." The name itself of " Moses " is obviously of Egyptian origin and was commonly used in the times of the Pharaohs. " *Mos*," or " *Mosh*," is the phonetic for the Egyptian sign *MS*, which expresses all kinds of ideas concerning birth and in particular that of " child." The Egyptians had the habit of putting their children under the protection of a certain god, even as we may call ours by the name of a saint. Thus, for example, we find such names as Ptah-Mos, " child of Ptah," Amon-Mos, " child of Amon," etc. . . .

The Bible states that the daughter of Pharaoh, finding a child floating in a basket on the waters of the Nile, " called his name Moses, *because*," she said, " *I drew him out of the water* " (Exod. ii, 2). This statement gives us the necessary clue to the primitive formation of the name of Moses which meant evidently : " Son of the Nile," or " Son of the waters." In the Egyptian tongue this would be either " Hapi-Mos " or " Mw-Mos." The words of the Bible stating that the name Moses was given to the child " *because* it was drawn out of the water " make this hypothesis quite obvious. It is also natural that Moses, after the exodus, and the creation of a new monotheistic religion, wanted to destroy all links that joined him to the ancient Egyptian gods, and therefore dropped the first part of his name, leaving only its termination, which did not convey to the imagination of his people any idea of the Egyptian pantheism.

The essence of the teaching which was at the core of the religion instituted by Moses was that which was taught in the Egyptian schools of initiation. This appears quite clearly from the study of the symbolic meaning of the ancient texts that we possess. It seems therefore natural to suppose that the first writing used by Moses was borrowed by him from his teachers, perhaps with some simplifications. But a great part of the teaching of Moses was not even put into writing and constituted the so-called " oral tradition " passed from one initiate to another in the course of his progress in the reception of spiritual teaching. The changes of fortune that characterised the first centuries of the life of the Hebrews made it necessary to form

H

their own writing and to incorporate in it, in a veiled and symbolic form, the essential principles of the primitive oral tradition, in order that it should not be utterly lost.

During the captivity in Babylon the primitive glyph was lost altogether and a new writing was created by the genius of the two prophets, Ezra and Daniel. The primitive teaching received from the Egyptian schools was subjected to the powerful influence of those that presented the doctrine of Assyria, and even the new alphabet was no more hieroglyphic but approached the cuneiform used in Mesopotamia in these days.

I must pass over many details which would necessitate a long study of the cuneiform writing. I will content myself with pointing out the principle on which the Hebraic writing was based and which was obviously borrowed from the cuneiforms.

All the Hebraic letters present a development of the letter " *Yod* " which entered into their formation, just as the sign of the *nail* (" *Til* " in the Babylonic writing) composes all the letters of the cuneiform alphabet. The idea and the phonetic of the letter " *Yod* " were both borrowed by the Hebrews from the Egyptian " *I*," the sign of the papyrus stem by the means of which the scribe traced the " words of god." But the fact that the Hebraic " *Yod* " enters *bodily* into the formation of every letter of the alphabet shows us that this idea was borrowed from the cuneiform writing.

The genius of the creators of the Hebraic writing consists in the fact that they rendered by means of a restricted number of twenty-two letters of the alphabet not only the phonetic sound characterising the tongue, but, by the considered composition of the different signs, gave the graphic representation of the different applications of forces of nature. Thus each letter of the Hebraic alphabet presents, apart from its phonetic meaning, a formula of a precise combination of constructive forces. We can thus understand the statement of the Book of Creation which says that God had created by the twenty-two letters "all that was created and all that is to be created." (*Sepher Ietzirah*, VI, 6.)

It may seem at the first glance that the composition of the Hebraic alphabet is much more simple than the Egyptian hieroglyph. This opinion is correct up to a certain point. To express their ideas the Egyptians used a great number of signs, the meanings of which, as I have pointed out, were partly ideographic, partly symbolic, and at the same time phonetic and grammatical. The Hebrews compressed all their knowledge within the narrow compass of twenty-two signs; thus, the rendering by them of the principles of creation had to be obviously precise and schematic. We know that the poorer the language is, the more it becomes necessary to express one's ideas with precision, and the more the correct choice of words becomes indispensable. In our days we see that for diplomatic relations between different countries the French language was chosen as the one that, being comparatively poor, necessitates naturally a great precision and a careful choice of wording, so as to avoid dangerous equivocations.

Though the Hebraic doctrine is expressed by the sole means of twenty-two conventional signs, it presents nevertheless a compound teaching which is comparable to a cut diamond reflecting light simultaneously from numerous facets.

The simplest and direct meaning, as was the case in the Egyptian texts, being intended for the general mass was so designed as to be at the level of the intelligence of a primitive man. It presented therefore a series of legends, or myths, and also concrete teaching concerning the organisation of society with its laws constituting the moral and sanitary life.

The symbolic meaning was intended for the initiate and exhibited the work of constructive forces of nature, combined in a precise formation to constitute the individuality of a particular form of creation. Thus it approached very closely the signification expressed by the symbolic meaning of the Egyptian hieroglyph.

But apart from that, the combination of certain letters of the Hebraic alphabet, taken in a precise order, presented ideographically (for the one who understood their formation) the particular combination of creative forces. This signification of the Hebraic letters can be traced in the twenty-two divine names that correspond to the twenty-two letters of the alphabet.

Apart from these two significations, each Hebraic letter presents simultaneously a number, and therefore a word, or a name can be judged also as a mathematical formula. The numeric meaning of the letters is expressed in the so-called Sephirothic decimal system. In the construction of this system the first ten letters of the alphabet have been taken and they present respectively in their natural order, the numbers from one to ten. I will devote one of the subsequent chapters to a consideration of this system, so now I will only give a general idea of it.

The Hebraic teaching inherited from Egypt the

idea of the synthetic unity (personified in the Egyptian religion by the God "Tem") which contains in potentiality all the following numbers considered as the consecutive divisions of the primordial One. The maximum of this division is the number *nine*. This idea was also inherited by the Hebrews from the Egyptian teaching and precisely from the Great Ennead considered as the maximum and definitive division of the Principle. There is not and cannot be a number greater than nine. It presents the accomplished analysis, the moment when the Primitive Unity has attained the maximum of its involutive penetration. The following number—ten—presents the return to the Unity in the next curve of the spiral of formation. Ten will be therefore *the unity of second degree*, the one that begins the "tens" and will develop until ninety in the image of the nine first numbers. The hundreds, the thousands and so on till infinity, will follow the same principle.

From the point of view of the first ten numbers, the tenth will present the zero, the return from the state of analysis to the state of synthesis, as on the face of a clock the end of the twelfth hour, the point zero presents the beginning of the first hour (as zero exists only theoretically).

Thus one understands that the Sephirothic system was composed of ten numbers only, corresponding to the first ten letters of the alphabet. It was considered sufficient to establish the idea of the cycle beginning by the "One," containing in potentiality all the following divisions and ending by the "One" containing their consecutive manifestation in reality. Therefore all the numbers can be reduced to the first nine numbers, and this reduction is usually called

" theosophical." I do not very well understand why the theosophists have appropriated this system which was known and employed long before the appearance of their teaching. One of the numerical systems of the Talmud is called " Ain-Becar," or the system of " nine squares," and its idea presents exactly the reduction of all the numbers of the alphabet to the primitive nine numbers.

I will give here a short example to illustrate what I have said, and to show the possibility of coexistence of three different meanings in one name.

The first, or more exactly, " Universal " man, is called in the book of Genesis Adam, written in Hebrew *Adm*. In the first meaning this word presents the phonetic of a name given to a man. In the symbolic meaning it is composed of the letters *Aleph*, that expresses the principal One, God the Creator of everything, who contains in Himself the potentiality of all possible life.

The next letter is *Daleth*, representing graphically the essential features of a cubic formation (its three measures seen in perspective), and symbolising the manifestation in reality of an idea. The idea of the cube presents the realisation in the world of three dimensions.

The last letter *Mem* expresses the idea of matter, or pro-matter (*Ma* the water, and simultaneously *Ma* the mother). This idea was also inherited by the Hebrews from the Egyptians where, as you remember, the sound *M* was rendered by the hieroglyph of the owl and meant symbolically the material envelope and formed the words meaning simultaneously : pro-matter, mother and death. It is curious to note that the symbolic image attached to the Hebraic letter

Mem in the so-called Great Arcana of the Tarot, which I will expound further—was "Death."

The tracing of the Hebraic letter *Mem* and also of the one belonging to the Samaritan transcription, as already pointed out, is practically the same as the one of another Egyptian hieroglyph rendering the same sound *M*. This letter represents graphically the joining (or the separation) of the waters above and the waters below, which, according to the Bible, constituted the formation of the sky and of the earth.

Thus, in the name Adam we see distinctly the union of two opposed principles: the spirit of God represented by the letter *Aleph* and the matter represented by the letter *Mem*. " And God formed man of the dust of the ground and breathed into his nostrils the breath of life." (Gen. ii, 7.)

The letter *Daleth* which in the name of Adam joins these two opposed principles presents, as I have said, the idea of a material formation generally submitted to the laws of the three dimensions.

But this is not all. The man, according to the teaching of the Bible, was the crown of Creation, the definite embodiment and culmination of the creative power, the last division of the unity, its development to the maximum. We find this idea expressed in the mathematic formula which is rendered by the name Adam judged from the point of view of its numeric composition. The letter *Aleph* corresponds to the number *one*, the letter *Daleth* is rendered by the number *four*, and the letter *Mem* by *forty*. Thus the name in question presents the total 45, or reduced to the primordial numbers, $4+5=9$. " Nine is the number of man, nine and not eight, nine and not ten." This number corresponds exactly to man as he is the last manifestation of God, his masterpiece, the culminating point of Creation. He is nine and not ten, as his life must evolve in the material plane and his work is precisely to conquer the attractions of the body, to rise out of the material plane and to gain reunion with the primitive Unity. He has got only one step to make, as the previous eight steps were made before him by the consecutive progress of nature manifested in the formation of the earth with all its inhabitants which preceded man and out of which he developed. Thus man has got to evolve from the state of nine to the state of ten, ten being the end of the cycle and the return to the Unity of God. This step might seem so short and so easy, and yet it presents all the terrible struggle that the spiritual part of man has to wage against the temptations of his body.

From this short example you can see what possibilities are opened up by a study of the Hebraic writing in its correct interpretation, though the writing itself seems at first glance so simple and solely phonetic in comparison with the Egyptian hieroglyphics.

The system employed by Moses in the composition of the book of Genesis was exactly the same as that which was employed by his Egyptian teachers. Under the form of simple and apparently childish legends the careful student will find a deep philosophic teaching unveiling the essential principles of Creation. It is not an exaggeration to say that all the discoveries of science made up to our day have their explanation in the wonderful book that is called " Genesis."

The translation of the Bible into Greek was effected by the order of Ptolomeos Lagos, who wanted to have it in his Alexandria library. This translation was made by five Esseians (learned men) and was approved as correct by the council of Seventy of Jerusalem. That is the reason why this translation received the name of " septuagint " (seventy).

It is natural that the interpreters who accomplished this translation used only the current, or as we call it, the *exoteric sense*, which was intended for the use of the uninitiated. The symbolic, or philosophic meaning was carefully protected, and reserved for the instruction of the initiates. This is the reason why the Bible in our opinion presents a book that expresses some elevated ideas in a more or less poetic or allegorical form.

The mistake of the authorities of different churches who consider the Bible as the basic book of their teaching is to accept it *to the letter* and not to admit any explanation which appears to them as being heretical. This point of view unfortunately created in our days a schism between religion and science which proves by its discoveries that the biblical statements do not correspond to the real facts. If, on the contrary, the leaders of our churches would admit that the statements of the Bible are expressed in a metaphorical way and that they must not be understood literally—all the opposition of so-called rational science would cease, and our children would not be left in a state of doubt which necessarily leads to unbelief and even to atheism.

For example, the six " days " of Creation must be understood as long periods, during which was gradually formed the material world. Thus the beginning of our globe, which according to the literal interpretation of the Bible was about seven thousand years ago, will be referred far back in time in agreement with the discoveries of the geologist, who possesses definite proof of the formation of the earth having occurred millions of years ago.

Many other points that are stated in the translation of the exoteric meaning of the Bible are misleading and are in contradiction with the discoveries of science—whereas they could be rightly interpreted by the careful study of the symbolic sense. Interpreted in their veiled and philosophic meaning, these statements would accord perfectly with the discoveries of science, and thus the two ways now opposed one to the other—the way of religion and the way of observation—would converge and confirm one another as it was in olden days.

A great French scholar, F. d'Olivet, has given in his wonderful book, *La Langue Hebraique restituée*, the correct interpretation of the symbolic meaning of the first ten chapters of the book of Genesis. The study of his book gives us a different and much more accurate idea of the real importance of the work of Moses. I cannot enter into details to establish this fact, as to do so would take me too far away from the direct object of the present chapter, so I advise all who want to study the question to read carefully the above-mentioned book.

I will give now a concise account of the composition of the Hebraic alphabet.

It is composed of twenty-two letters, presenting three cycles, each of seven letters, and one (the last one) synthetic letter which simultaneously presents the zero, or, as I said, the return to the primordial Unity. It is interesting to remark here that the number 22 corresponds exactly to the same number of sounds of the Egyptian phonetic alphabet. The only difference is that the twenty-two Egyptian sounds were rendered by means of twenty-six letters, as some of the sounds were represented by two different signs (one corresponding to the macrocosmos and the other to the microcosmos).

The number 22 contains an important idea of the totality of creative forces in their full development. I will come back to this essential number in the chapter concerning numerology.

The twenty-two letters of the Hebraic alphabet are constituted as follows: three " mothers," seven " doubles," and twelve " simple." The three " mothers " form the basic principle of Trinity, or, as I have explained previously, the equilibriated division. They also correspond respectively to the three planes: mental (*Aleph*), astral or animic (*Mem*), and physical, or of definite manifestation of the creative power (*Shin*). *Aleph* is the first letter of the alphabet and corresponds to the Creative Reason. *Mem* is the thirteenth letter and corresponds to Death, or to transformation. *Shin* is the twenty-first letter, the one that terminates the third cycle of definite manifestation, the involution after which follows inevitably the evolution marked by the twenty-second and last letter—the zero.

The seven " doubles " are so called because each of them symbolises a quality and a corresponding defect. For example, intelligence and stupidity, fecundity and sterility, etc. Thus the influence of these letters can be considered in the limits constituted by its own + and its —.

In the macrocosmos the seven doubles correspond to the seven planets, and in the microcosmos—to the features of the human face, or abstractly to the senses of man. Thus two letters—*Beth* and *Caph*, govern

PLATE V

Sign.	No.	Phonetic	Ideographic Meaning.	Universe.	Man.	Symbolic Meaning.	Sephiroth.	Tarot.	Name of God.
א	1	A	Action—counter-action—equilibrium	Spiritual world	Chest	The man	Kheter	The Mage	Ehieh
ב	2	B	First division, reflection	☽	Right eye	Science	Chochma	The gate of the temple	Bachur
ג	3	G	The channel	♀	Right ear	Action	Binah	Isis Uranis	Gadol
ד	4	D	The cube	♃	Right nostril	Realisation	Chezed	The cubic stone	Dagoul
ה	5	Hé	Application of man's work	♈	Right leg	Inspiration	Gheburah	The master of arcanes	Hadom
ו	6	W, U	The separating and joining power	♉	Right kidney	The proof The test	Tiferet	The two ways	Vezio
ז	7	Z	The joining power	♊	Left leg	The victory	Nezach	The chariot	Zakaï
ח	8	H	The field of action	♋	Right arm	Equilibrium	Hod	Thémis	Chased
ט	9	T	The roof	♌	Left kidney	Prudence	Yezod	The veiled lamp	Fehor
י	10	Y	The index	♍	Left arm	Fortune	Malcut	The Sphinx	Yah

Hebrew	No.	Letter	Word	Symbol	Body part	Quality	Description	Divine name
ך	20	K	The mould	♂	Left eye	Strength	The lion	Mittatron
ל	30	L	The wing	♎	Bile	Violent death	The sacrifice	Saday
מ	40	M	The woman	Astral world	Intestines	Transformation	Death	Jehovah
נ	50	N	The fruit	♏	Bowels	Human initiative	The genius	Emmanuel
ס	60	S	The serpent	♐	Stomach (Keva)	Fatality	Typhon	Sameek
ע	70	O	The place	♑	Liver	Ruin	The ruined tower	Jehovah Zebaoth
פ	80	P, Ph	The mouth and the tongue	☿	Left ear	Hope	The star of Magi	Phode
צ	90	Tz	The attacking serpent	♒	Stomach (Ker Kova)	Deception	The dawn	Tsedeck
ק	100	Q	The hatchet	♓	The spleen	Happiness	The light	Kodesh
ר	200	R	The head	♄	Left nostril	Renewal	The awakening of the dead	Rodesh
ש	300	Sh	The fire	Physical world	Head of the man	Expiation	The crocodile	Shadai
ת	400	Th	The logos	☉	Mouth	Recompense	The crown	Techinach

the two eyes, *Daleth* and *Resh*—the two nostrils, *Phe* and *Gimel*—the two ears, and the letter *Tau* reigns over the mouth.

The twelve " simple " present the frame in which evolves the life of the Universe and particularly of man. Thus they correspond in the macrocosmos to the twelve signs of the Zodiac, and in the body of man to his internal organs and his limbs. These correspondences indicate the different influences that man receives from the combined forces of Nature, and the study of these influences presents the ancient science called astrology. The Zodiacal circle constitutes the boundaries in which evolves the Universe, and for man the twelve corresponding letters express the world of natural forces in his body which act without the control of his reason (thus they cannot express either a quality or a defect like the seven doubles).

These last represent in the macrocosmos the precise combination of influences which form the particular being of man and the development of life in general. In man they present the precise combination of his individuality and are submitted to the action of his reason and will-power. It is he himself who makes the choice between the two limits posited by the double letter and either evolves his spirituality, or involves it in to the depths of matter.

To conclude, I will repeat in short that a name or any word written in letters of the Hebraic alphabet can be considered : (1) in its direct or phonetic meaning ; (2) in the symbolic sense expressing the generation idea that was at the basis of the precise formation ; (3) as a graphic representation of the different forces of nature combined in a particular and purely individual way ; (4) and last, the word can

PLATE VI

1. ≬ Iod.

2. Ⓢ Yn-Yang.

3. □ The precise forma-
tion fixed and unmov-
able.

4. ◇ The same in move-
ment.

5. △ The Ternary evolved
out of One.

6. ∧ The Ternary created
by the equilibrated
division of the principle
One in Two.

7. The elements enter-
ing in the formation
of the letter Aleph.
Compare with the
Egyptian sign ⌢ᶜ
passivity; and with
⌢ᶜ existence.

8. א Aleph decomposed
into its elements and
showing the shock given
to the horizontal line
which carries it out of
its state of passivity, and

gives as a result birth to
the second Iod.

9. ב Beth which evolves
into כ Caph and מ
Mem; compare with the
Samaritan Mem ⌇⌇⌐
and with the Egyptian
⌐ M.

10. ג Ghimel developed
out of: י Iod; ו
Vau, and precised in
the manifestation of נ
—Noun—the child.

11. ד Daleth, the idea of
the cube in its three
dimensions ⌂

12. מ Mem decomposed
into its elements ב—
Beth and ו—Vau.

13. ש מ א — Schma —
the scheme containing
in itself all the elements
of creation.

14. י ה ו The spiritual
Ternary evolving into
its realisation in the
quaternary which is ex-
pressed in יחוה the
name Tetragrammaton.

15. א ד מ—Adam.

be judged as a mathematical formula presenting the essence of the name of a being, or of an object. A still deeper penetration into the spiritual sense of a letter, and therefore of a word, can be obtained by the study of the Divine name or names attached to every letter.

But this is not all. There exists yet another system based on the knowledge of the Hebraic alphabet, that is called the " Tarot " or the " Great Arcana." This system presents twenty-two symbolical pictures each corresponding to a precise letter. The conventional drawing of these pictures is based on the ancient principle of ideography combined with symbolism. Each picture or card of the Tarot contains a revelation of the most profound initiation. The origin of these conventional pictures has been the subject of much discussion and disputation, and it would take too long a time to enter into such details. It will be sufficient to say that we can trace the symbolism of the Tarot to the so-called " Keys of Solomon " in which was hidden the teaching of the ancient oral tradition. Perhaps one could trace some of the Tarot symbols still farther to their Egyptian origin.

This wonderful symbolic " picture book " gave the idea for the construction of our trivial pack of cards, by means of which the medieval sorcerers told fortunes. The first game played with the Tarot cards had the mysterious name of " The shadow of man."

I will return to the consideration of the Great Arcana in the course of this book, as even a short and schematic exposition of their symbolism would necessitate too long a digression.

CHAPTER II

THE TERNARY—EQUILIBRIUM

THOUGH the hieroglyphic language is much more complicated than the Hebraic writing, the teaching that is given by the latter is perhaps more difficult to be understood correctly and necessitates the greatest attention. This is due to the fact that the Hebraic teaching is more concise and more abstract than its Egyptian prototype. Also, the ideographic sign of the hieroglyphic writing helps a great deal towards the understanding of the ideas of the Egyptian doctrine.

I will try to unfold before you the mysteries of the Hebraic teaching as clearly as possible, without entering into too many details, so that you may be able to follow the development of the general idea.

In the present chapter we will study the manner in which the principle of Creation manifested itself in its first division, in which the two opposite elements had necessarily to be equilibrated, one in regard to the other. This equilibrated division, as I have said before, formed the basic principle of ternary, or Trinity, which laid the foundation of most developed religions.

This idea was rendered in the Egyptian teaching by the formula *Mout-F* (mother-father), and in the Cabala by the " Balance that was in the Ancient of Days."

The first ternary of the Hebraic teaching is rendered by the three letters called the " mothers " which are *Aleph*, *Mem*, and *Shin*, and also by the first three letters of the alphabet: *Aleph*, *Beth*, and *Gimel*, representing numerically the first three numbers.

Before starting the study of the particular ideas attached to these letters, I will submit a short review of the formation of the Hebraic letters in general and of the first three letters in particular.

At the basis of the formation of all the Hebraic letters was the letter *Iod*. This letter enters bodily into every one of the letters of the alphabet, presenting its starting-point, or in other words, its principle. Graphically, the letter *Iod* presents a point, or more precisely a sort of comma. Drawn largely, the *Iod* will constitute a centre which is formed by two elements, or two spirals joined together. The idea that was in the formation of this sign was suggested by the grain at the moment of sprouting. Thus it presents a centre throwing out simultaneously a growth and a root. The Chinese rendered the same idea by the sign *Yn-Yang*, in which, in one circle, are combined two elements closely joined together. This sign presents the prototype of the primitive division of a material cell, but also constitutes a precise manifestation which has descended from a previous formation, but bears in itself the germ which will form a new life. The plant " yielding fruit, whose seed was in itself after its kind " . . . to give birth to a new specimen of the same kind. Therefore the grain is a very appropriate symbol for conveying the above-mentioned idea, as by one end (its root) it maintains its present life, and by its growth it forms a new plant, which will bear the same kind of grain in its time. Thus the grain became naturally the symbol of eternity, or more exactly, of the eternal nature of life, and of its resurrection out of death.

Numerically, the letter *Iod* represents the number ten, or as I have said already, " the unity of second degree," the manifestation in life of the principle of unity enounced by the first letter of the alphabet— *Aleph*. One will understand, therefore, the role that was appointed to the letter *Iod* in the Hebraic teaching, which considered it as the *creative unity*, the one of formation of all phenomena of manifested life. Thus you will understand the reason why the sign by which was traced this letter entered into the formation of all the other letters of the alphabet.

Apart from the letter *Iod*, two other elements enter into the composition of the glyph of the so-called " square " Hebraic letter. One is the vertical line and the other is the horizontal line. The vertical line symbolises an active force which can have a double action : either from up downwards, or in the opposite direction—upwards. The first will express the involutive penetration and the second the evolutive elevation. I remind you that the Egyptian sign of the human leg (letter *B*) had exactly the same double function, which is clearly rendered in the words *BN* (perpendicular) and *NB* (elevation of the plane). The horizontal line is the sign of passivity and this idea was also borrowed by the Hebrews from the Egyptian symbolism which expressed it by the sign of the surface of the water (letter *N*).

A third element is the inclined line, the one that came out of the state of stability, of the horizontal plane by the action, or a shock received from some external force. This inclined line does not symbolise itself as a force, but a *received movement*, expressing the idea of something that became animated. Therefore, for example, in the symbolic sign language, a square will express the idea of a precise formation not having in it any movement or life, and a lozenge will show a movement of some kind which animates its formation. The triangle (constituting one of the faces of the Pyramid) reposes on a solid basis—the horizontal line, and its two slanting sides, converging to one point at the summit represent graphically the emanation by the Principle One of two different constructive powers. From the point of view of man who has built a pyramid on the solid basis of the earth, the lateral faces of the triangle, ascending to meet in the summit, symbolise the dominant idea of the builder oriented towards the elevation to the Principle. The Egyptian pyramid expressed precisely this idea, thus the name of this edifice, meaning literally " the coming out towards birth," is quite appropriate and illuminating.

After this short exposition of the principles of symbolic signs, I hope that the formation of the letters of the Hebraic alphabet will become comprehensible.

The first letter of this alphabet is *Aleph*, and it represents graphically the active Principle One manifested by *Iod*, producing its action upon the passive surface—the horizontal line. This first shock throws the surface out of the state of horizontal (passivity), into the state of incline (movement), and as a consequence of this first movement, there results a new manifestation represented by the second *Iod*. Thus the glyph of the letter *Aleph* represents graphically the idea that the Principle One bears in itself the ternary, or in other words the scheme of all subsequent creation.

Taken separately, the three elements forming the letter *Aleph* remind us of the idea expressed by the Egyptians in the name of pro-matter *NW* and the one of existence *WN*.

According to the book of Creation (*Sepher Ietzirah*) the three first manifestations of the creative power form the three principal elements of nature : the breath, the water, and the fire. " The water (is formed) out of the breath . . . the fire—out of water. . . ." (*Seph. Ietz.*, I, II, 12.) Thus in the glyph *Aleph* the water is symbolised by the horizontal line, the breath by the first *Iod* which gave the shock to the line, changing its horizontal position into the inclined one. At last the fire is symbolised by the second *Iod*. The creating breath has thrown the surface out of the state of passivity (horizontal), and from the shock was born fire.

I cannot go deeper into this analysis as it would necessitate too much explanation and I have got many other points to explain in order to give a general idea of the Hebraic teaching concerning the ternary.

Symbolically, the letter *Aleph* as a whole presents the Principle One (*Tem-Mout-F*) ; the idea containing in itself all the following forms of creation ; the male that contains in himself the germ which will generate all the consecutive generations ; the principle of life in its eternal development (" *I am one* who became two, four, eight—but *I am one*. . . .").

The second letter of the alphabet, representing numerically the number two, is *Beth*. This letter corresponds in the macrocosmos to the moon, to the reflection of the principle of life, to the female as the companion of the male. It represents the first division of the Principle One, when the dividing power has separated its essence into two parts. Thus its glyph represents graphically this idea. We see in the tracing of this letter the two parallel horizontal lines, the lower one—the foundation, the base, " the waters below," to which is joined by a vertical line the upper one representing " the waters above." This constitutes the first division of pro-matter mentioned in the book of Genesis.

The two horizontal lines joined by a vertical line are, according to the expounded principles of symbolic representations, " without movement "—thus this letter constitutes *the idea of division*, but not the actual dividing power. We can therefore relate the idea expressed by this letter to the first division personified by the gods *Shou* and *Tefnut* of the Egyptian teaching. The vertical line which joins the two horizontal lines in the letter *Beth* will have in it a double current which will depend on the orientation of the idea : upwards to express the elevation, the evolutive movement ; or downwards to render the involution, the penetration of the vivifying principle into the depths of matter. In the metaphoric representation by this letter of the division of " waters above " and " waters below " it will be : *the mist* " which went up from the earth " (Gen. ii, 6), and the rain that falls from the sky and " waters all the face of the earth."

The next development of the idea of division will be shown in the letter *Caph*=20, the penetration of the force of division, its manifestation of the second degree ; and *Mem*=40, the water, the mother element in which the cycle of exchange has formed itself and is graphically represented by the addition to the previous sign of a new element—a *Yod*, representing the principle of life which animates the cycle. The letter *Mem* will therefore correspond in the Egyptian teaching to the second couple of divinities, *Geb* and *Nut*, which form the natural frame in which evolve all the created individualities.

The third letter of the alphabet is *Gimel*. Numerically it represents the number three, and symbolically it expresses the idea of the link which joins together the two elements of the first division. Graphically, this letter is composed of the sign of the creative principle *Yod* which emanates out of himself a power —the vertical line. Thus is created the sign of the letter *Vau*, which symbolically expresses the idea of " joining together," and at the same time of " separating " two distinct elements formed out of the first division of the Unity. It joins them for the manifestation of their union necessary for the generation of a new life, but it separates them one from another, not allowing each of them to lose its particular individuality. Thus the role of this letter is the same as the one of the Egyptian hieroglyphic sign *T* employed in the formula *Mout-F*, which joins the two parents for the formation of a child, but which at the same time defines each of them as a separate individual.

In the letter *Gimel*, which interests us for the moment, the vertical line emanated by the Principle (*Yod*) meets on its way of penetration an element (represented graphically by another *Yod*) with which it enters into a relation of some sort. This relation does not yet constitute a precise and definite manifestation—idea that is clearly represented by the fact that the vertical line only *touches* this second *Yod* on its way and continues its further penetration. The real and precise formation, the child, is constituted in the letter *Nun*, in which we see the vertical line *stopped* in its movement of penetration by the second *Yod* forming the base of the new letter. Here the first *Yod*, which generated the movement, represents symbolically the parents, the root of the grain ; and the second *Yod* to which the first is joined by the vertical line, represents the child, the fruit, the growth which sprouted from the grain.

In the letter *Gimel* the vertical line represents the force of penetration, *the current from above*, emanated by the Principle (*Yod*). In the letter *Nun* the same line possesses a *double current*, representing the natural exchange between two distinct elements—the parents and the child, or the root and the growth. This double current characterises every particular manifestation of life in an individual formation.

Thus the letter *Gimel* symbolises *the potentiality of a child* as a natural result of the union of the two parents, and the letter *Nun* presents the actual *formation of the child* as a separate individual.

Abstractly the letter *Gimel* expresses the idea of the deduction made by the reason of man (symbolised by *Aleph*) after it had studied and understood a precise manifestation by the means of its faculty of understanding (*cognito*), symbolised by the letter *Beth* (the reflector).

The first numerical ternary of the Hebraic teaching can be therefore represented graphically. The essential point is that both letters (*Beth* and *Gimel*) are emanated from the principle and *not created successively*. The Principle One possessed the idea of the division in himself (the Balance in the Ancient of Days) and started the creation by the manifestation of this principle of division. This idea in the Egyptian teaching is rendered in the simultaneous birth from *Ra* of the first couple, *Shou* and *Tefnut*, symbolising the two principal powers of creation : the power of expansion and the power of limitation.

The same idea was rendered in the Gospel, where it is said that " the Holy Ghost descendeth from the Father " and *not from the Father and the Son*. The introduction in the Latin " Credo " of the words " Filioque " was a great mistake, which shows that those who composed it did not understand the basic idea of the Christian teaching and reduced the Trinity to its most trivial interpretation requiring two elements to create a third. Thus according to the definition of the Catholic Church, the Son corresponds to the female element of a pagan divine family—the mother who joins herself to the father in order to give life to the child.

This form of expressing the idea of ternary was necessarily employed by the primitive religions in order to convey to the unprepared mind of man the abstract idea under an acceptable and comprehensive form. But this is only a materialistic form and it wrongs the real sense of the primitive idea. Neither Christ, nor the initiates of the ancient schools intended this meaning for the revelation of the basic idea of creation, which is emanated from *One Unique Principle*, rendered by the Egyptians in the hieroglyphic *Tem*— the reason of life.

As I have said, the first three letters of the Hebraic alphabet constitute the first three numbers of the numeric system. Each of them presents separately a particular number, and all together they form the ternary. Without one of them this formation is incomplete, and it is the letter *Aleph* (the unity) that gives the possibility of passing from one element to another, or as the texts say : " *Aleph* is the law that establishes the equilibrium " between the other two. Mathematically, one sees that each of these three numbers is formed by the addition of the unity (*Aleph*) to the previous letter ($2 = 1 + 1$, $3 = 2 + 1$).

To express the material formation of the world as well as of man, the Hebraic alphabet used another ternary constituted by the three " mothers "—*Aleph*, *Mem*, and *Shin*. These letters correspond respectively to the mental, astral, and physical worlds.

Mathematically, these letters express the numbers : 1, 40, and 300. As you see, the reduction of these three numbers to the primitive nine gives the sum 8 ($1 + 4 + 3 = 8$). Thus they represent in their totality the eight elements obtained by the consecutive division of the primordial unity personified by the eight gods of the Egyptian Ennead, or the eight divisions of Ra (" I am eight "). As I have said, *Aleph* is the Principle One, containing in potentiality all the divisions to be, thus it presents naturally the number one. *Mem* is the thirteenth letter of the alphabet and expresses numerically the number 40. It is therefore a penetration of second degree of the basic number four, the one that expresses the idea of a precise manifestation in reality. But as I have said in the previous chapter, the whole of the Hebraic alphabet is based upon the formation of *three cycles*, or degrees in which develops the creative power. The first cycle is the one of *Principle* (or spirit), the second—the one of *constructive forces* (or astral), and the third is the one of *manifestation* of phenomena (or physical reality).

Thus the letter *Mem*, belonging to the second degree of penetration, presents the organisation of constructive forces ready to produce the phenomena, *but is not yet the phenomena itself.* It is, if one allows me to use this word, the so-called astral body of a being, but not its physical body. The number four that forms the constructive idea in the first degree from which is evolved the number 40, expresses a definite formation of the constructive power *in principle.* Thus the number 40 will signify also the definite organisation of forces, or in other words, the construction of the astral body which will in the following cycle be enveloped in a material shape.

The numerical meaning of the third " mother " *Shin* is 300. It belongs therefore to the third cycle of penetration of the involutive force which begins by 100. The number three which constitutes the principle of the number 300 expresses, as you know, the law of equilibrium, the ternary. It does not convey the idea of definite construction like the following number four, but is immaterial and abstract. As you remember, the law of ternary is at the base of all the ancient teaching and expresses the dynamism of life, dynamism which is stabilised, or fixed by the quaternary, the cube. Thus the number three in its third state of development (300) expresses the idea of penetration of the creative power to the bottom of things, the readiness of the preparatory work to manifest itself in a precise phenomena in the physical world (which will be expressed by the number 400).

Therefore you will understand that the sum composed by these three letters (*Aleph, Mem, Shin*) is *eight* and not nine. It is the complete development of the forces of division, the being containing in potentiality the principle (reason), the definite formation of the constructive forces (astral body, or will), and the development of the physical construction. It is like the plan and all the necessary material which will be employed for the building of a house, but that are not yet the house itself.

The idea of a definite construction is given, as I have said, by the number four, thus the construction itself will be rendered by the penetration of the same number in its third stage, or in other words, by the number 400. This last number corresponds to the letter *Tau*, the one of definite accomplishment of the Creation and corresponds therefore to man—the crown of all the work of the Creator. In the number eight are represented all the forces working for the construction of the world, and their work is purely involutive, presenting the consecutive divisions of the primordial Unity. The number nine represents man (Adam), who is the last stroke, the masterpiece of the Creator, and thus personifies the penetration of the involutive or analytic force to the bottom. But in the same time man possesses the evolutive force and his reason, apart from the analysis, is capable of understanding the synthesis.

In man the first part of the cycle of Creation is accomplished and the second part begins the return towards the principle, the synthetic work of reducing to the unity all the innumerable particles of division The choice of the way of return, as well as a greater or lesser intenseness of the progress, depends on the free will of man. One understands therefore that the first nine numbers must be followed by the number ten, the unity of second degree, the return to the Principle. The last, twenty-second letter of the alphabet, which follows the realisation of the third cycle (21), is *Tau*, corresponding simultaneously to the number 400—the definite manifestation of the creative power, and to zero—the end of the cycle, the return to the beginning.

I hope that this rather difficult discussion unveils clearly enough one of the principal ideas which are at the base of the Hebraic teaching.

From the physical point of view the " mother " letters correspond respectively in the macrocosmos : *Aleph*—to the air, *Mem*—to the water, and *Shin*—to the fire. " The sky is created of fire, the earth of water, and the air out of the breath, and holds the place between them." (*Sepher Ietzirah*, III, 3.) This statement of the book of Creation is, as you can judge, of pure Egyptian origin and renders in words the graphic representation of *Shou* (the god of the air) separating the sky from the earth. You remember also that it is said in the Egyptian texts concerning *Shou* that " he was born from the breath of Ra."

For the body of man, concerning the three letters, it is said :

" The head is created out of fire (*Shin*), the abdomen out of water (*Mem*), and the chest out of ether (*Aleph*), and holds the equilibrium between them " (ibid., III, 4).

The philosophic idea of the trinity of formation was expressed in the mysterious name of three letters : *Iod-He-Vau* ; in which is combined the essence of the whole Hebraic teaching. This name is composed of the active principle (*Iod*), the passive principle (*He*), and the one that joins them together and at the same time separates each of them one from the other, which is rendered by the letter *Vau*. I have expounded these essential principles, when I analysed the basic idea of Trinity. The three above-mentioned letters enter into the construction of the great name " *IEVE*," called Tetragrammaton—" the name of four letters." This name contains schematically all the essential ideas of the ancient teaching. The three letters constitute the principle of ternary, the addition of a fourth element expresses the so-called " passage from the state of ternary to the state of quaternary," or in other words, from the state of formative forces to the state of reality of phenomena. The fact that the fourth element added to the ternary presents the repetition of one of the constituting elements (the second *He*), strengthens the idea that all the constructive powers necessary for the formation of a precise manifestation enter into the constitution of the ternary, which presents all possible manifestation in the state of potentiality.

The Trinity is therefore the complete expression of all possibilities of creation and *nothing can be added to it that would not be already in it*. The realisation of the formative forces presents only their stabilisation, their fixing in a precise state. This idea is rendered in the name Tetragrammaton by the addition to the formating ternary of the second *He*, or in other words, of the passive element. The idea is the same as the one expressed in the Egyptian writing where for a precise formation, or fixation of a movement in a definite and unmovable state, one added the letter *N* symbolising the plane, the passiveness.

As I have said already, the symbol corresponding to the idea of ternary in the symbolic sign language was the triangle, and the sign corresponding to the quaternary was the square. Thus in the name Tetragrammaton we see the combination of these two ideas : the ternary constituted by the three first letters, and the quaternary expressed by the repetition of the letter *He*. The name Tetragrammaton was considered as the essential formula of creation and thus possessed the greatest power for one who understood it and knew how to use it. This name could not be pronounced by the uninitiate, who called it " Tetragrammaton." Only the high priest had the right to pronounce this name, and this he accomplished in a fashion that its pronunciation could not be caught by anyone in the crowd.

The transposition of letters forming this name presents the scheme of all possible transpositions of letters, or in other terms, the different combinations of the creative forces combined in order to form all possible manifestations of real life.

There existed a whole branch of science which studied the transpositions of letters, which were executed according to different elaborated systems. This science is based upon the following text : " How did He (God) trace them and (how did He) effect the combinations and the transpositions ? One letter with all and all the letters with one, two letters with all and all with two and so on. . . . Thus everything that was created and all the verb have got the same origin." (*Sepher Ietzirah*, II, 5.) And elsewhere concerning the ten numbers which represent the Sephirothic system : " Understand by your sense of comprehension and conceive by your sense of understanding ; test them, scrutinise them, put them each as it is necessary and place the Creator in His place." (Ibid., I, 4.)

This *correct disposition* of the creative powers symbolised under the form of the twenty-two letters represents the so-called *Rota*, or " wheels of the creation."

These wheels turn round the centre which is One ; every slightest turn manifests itself in the transformation of the creative ternary into its reflection—the quaternary, and both forming together the number of the universal gamut (seven).

The whole of this movement produces itself in the frame of the twelve signs which tint by their particular influences the formation created by the movements of the Rota.

Thus the principal *One* develops into the equilibrated division—*three*, and the next basic numbers —seven and twelve—present only the further application of the idea posed by the ternary. " God alone is above the three, three are above the seven, seven is above the twelve ; and all are joined between themselves." (*Sepher Ietzirah*, IV, 5.)

Every possible manifestation of life is contained in potentiality in the Unity of the Creator, and the unique law that rules the universe is expressed in the idea of the *ternary-equilibrium*. All the other laws present only different forms of application of this sole law of equilibrium. That is the reason why this idea was put at the basis of all developed religions in the form of the mysterious Trinity.

Just a last remark before concluding this chapter. The word " scheme " employed by all Occidental languages to express the idea of outlining a thing in its essential features—is nothing less than the three Hebraic letters *Shin-Mem-Aleph* (*SHMA*), the three " mothers," containing in them " schematically " all the ideas concerning the constructive powers of the whole alphabet. " He (God) created by the combination Shin-Mem-Aleph the head in the body of man." (*Sepher Ietzirah*, III, 8.) We know that the human head, according to the teaching of the ancients, schematised man in his whole totality. In the Egyptian texts we often meet the expression " faces " (*Hru*) employed instead of " men." Thus when we employ the word " *schema* " we unconsciously refer to the ternary principle of the Hebraic alphabet.

CHAPTER III

THE SEPTENARY AND THE DUODENARY

THE detailed study of the Hebraic writing in order to extract the totality of the ideas that are expressed by it, must be carried out on the following lines.

1. The tracing of the glyph gives the scheme of the constructive forces of Nature, combined in a particular way so as to create definite phenomena, which will express the formation of a name. The letters, entering into its combination in a particular order, define the being, or the object named. Thus one can say that this study reveals the formula of construction of the being, or object named, and therefore approaches the ideographic meaning of the signs in the primitive tongues.

2. Each letter, apart from its phonetic sound, possesses a particular nomenclature. For example, the first letter of the alphabet—expressing the sound of an aspiration, which is rendered in our language by the vowels *A* or *E*—is called *Aleph*. The second letter corresponding to our *B* has the name *Beth*; the third answering to our *C* is named *Gimel*, and so on. As you see from these few examples, the " name " of a letter begins by the sound which characterises its phonetic. But the composition of the particular nomenclature of a letter enlarges and completes the

meaning revealed by the design of the glyph which it denominates.

3. The place that the letter occupies in the alphabet has also great importance. It shows the *rank* that the letter in question occupies in the cycle of creative forces, and expresses the stage of development attained by the creative power in its work of formation of the universe and of man in particular.

4. The numerical meaning of a letter represents its mathematical signification and allows the construction of a word in the form of a mathematic formula. The number expressed by the letter is different from its rank in the alphabet mentioned in the previous paragraph. These two numbers are the same only for the first ten letters—the Sephiroths. For the following letters, the number of a letter will present the sum of the numbers of its rank taken at a further stage. Thus, for example, the eleventh letter of the alphabet will present the number 20 $(1+1)$, the thirteenth letter will be forty $(1+3)$, and so on.

5. The so-called Sephiroths constitute the decimal system which is incorporated in the Hebraic alphabet, representing a part of the twenty-two letters, as the Sephiroths are attached to the first ten letters of the alphabet. But at the same time the Sephirothic system presents a distinct teaching apart from the alphabet and forming a particular and complete cycle of its own. This idea is rendered in the Cabala by the so-called system of " thirty-two ways," by which one obtained revelations. One sees that this new system is composed of the twenty-two letters of the alphabet, to which are added the ten Sephiroths, which in this case are considered as being separate from the cycle of twenty-two letters $(32=22+10)$.

Each Sephirah possesses a particular name, and it is this name that expresses the so-called "attribute" of God which the Sephirah represents. Thus, for example, the name of the first Sephirah corresponding to the letter *Aleph* is "*Kether*," meaning the "crown," the second Sephirah is "*Chochma*," and so on. As you see, these names are totally different from the names of the letters and even do not contain the phonetic sound which characterises the letter to which they correspond. The study of the nomenclature of the Sephiroths gives a new revelation concerning the particular work of the creative power of God. All the letters of the alphabet are closely related to the Sephiroths presenting either their direct application (in the first ten letters), or their reflection in a more or less deep way. For example, the letter *Caph* which represents numerically twenty, is the extension in the second degree of the Sephirah "*Chochma*," corresponding to the letter *Beth*. And we see that the sign by which is represented the letter *Beth* is closely allied to the one rendering the letter *Caph*. Both of them express ideographically the *reflection*. The first (*Beth*) is the particular sign of the principle of division : the woman in regard to man, the moon in regard to the sun. The letter *Caph* represents graphically the mould in which is fashioned a particular formation. The third state of extension of the Sephirah "*Chochma*" is the letter *Resh*, numerically 200, which expresses the maximum of the extension of the dividing power signified by the letter *Beth*. *Resh* creates, according to Kircher, the "life of plants," or in other words the vegetative power of Nature with which begin all the manifestations of life.

6. For the macrocosmos each letter corresponds

either to a planet (the " double " letters), or to a sign of the Zodiac (the " simple " letters), thus it expresses the particular influence which is characterised by the corresponding star.   For the microcosmos it will express a particular part of the human body.   The study of this part of the alphabet finds its application in astrology and in the medical art.

7. Each letter is related to a particular *Arcanum*, or symbolic picture, in which is hidden under the form of a conventional image the revelation of the oral tradition.   Thus, for example, the first letter corresponds to the Arcanum representing the *Magus*, the reasonable being possessing knowledge, and the power to make use of his knowledge, which he directs towards his predestined evolution.

8. To each letter is attached a rank of angelic forces, the emissaries of God, by whose agency the creative Principle has built and rules the Universe.

9. At last the highest revelation is given by the twenty-two names of God which are attached respectively to every letter of the alphabet and interpret them in the highest spiritual way.

You will understand, from this short exposition, that the study of all the ideas attached to the twenty-two letters of the Hebraic alphabet necessitates deep concentration and presents a task requiring long and arduous toil.   It is utterly impossible to expound the essence of this marvellous teaching in the course of a few short chapters, as even an incomplete study of the principles on which it is based required numerous long treatises written by scholars of different epochs. I will therefore content myself with outlining in the most general terms the possibilities which the study of the Hebraic alphabet can open up to a zealous student. Those who are interested in a particular branch of these studies may consult many remarkable works written in different languages and at different epochs. But I repeat that the study of all these works requires long and assiduous labour, and only on this condition is it possible to obtain some perceptible results.

Now I will proceed to outline the ideas concerning the septenary and the duodenary which are revealed by the Hebraic teaching, and obtained from an analysis of the alphabet of twenty-two letters. In the preceding chapter I stated that the principal law on which is based all Creation is that of *equilibrium*, expressed by the ternary or Trinity.

The next law that rules the world is that of the universal gamut. This second law is evolved immediately from that of the ternary, as the latter presents the first division of the Unity. " God alone is above the three, and three are above the seven." (*Sepher Ietzirah*, VI, 5.)

Thus, as the Trinity is derived from the Unity, the seven is based on the principle of equilibrium enunciated by the Trinity. " Out of the seven—three are against three, and one fixes the equilibrium between them." (Ibid., VI, 5.) In the seven we must therefore consider two ternaries judged each as a unity, and opposed one to the other. The seventh element will present the point of equilibrium in regard to these two opposing ternaries-unities.

In the macrocosmos, the number seven corresponds to the six planets of our system known to antiquity. The seventh element, the centre, corresponds to the sun round which revolve the six planets : Venus, Mercury, the Moon, Saturn, Jupiter, and Mars. The particular influences of these planets combined together in a precise way constitute the formation of a particular individual in whom the combination of these influences equilibrates itself in one way or another. " God opposed one thing against another " (Eccles. vii, 14); " the good against the evil and the evil against the good ; the good (proceeds) from the good, and the evil—from the evil ; the good puts to test the evil, and the evil (does the same) for the good." (*Sepher Ietzirah*, VI, 4.)

Thus we come back to the combined work of the opposed forces of nature, which was symbolised in the Egyptian mythology by the continued struggle between *Horus* and *Seth*, or between the forces of expansion and the forces of limitation, personified by the first couple (*Shou* and *Tefnut*) of the Egyptian pantheon.

Theoretically, in the seven elements composing the universal gamut, the equilibrium is first created in each group of three elements, which are then judged as a unity and are opposed one to the other. This opposition constitutes the second stage of equilibrium formed by the seventh element of the gamut. This definite result will theoretically be *perfect* equilibrium. Practically, the latter does not exist and the continuous struggle of opposed forces presents life in its ups and downs when either the forces of evil, or the forces of good prevail, or are conquered at a certain moment.

The idea of equilibrium is rendered by the double nature of the seven " double " letters of the alphabet, each of them possessing simultaneously a particular quality and a corresponding opposite quality. The influence radiated by forces represented by the letter oscillates between these two extremities, thus the particular influence of a letter is equilibrated in itself and every " double " letter can be judged as a ternary with its own + and its specific −, which equilibrate themselves about a certain point. This point is not necessarily in the centre, and on the contrary can be displaced in regard to the more or less positive or negative general emanation. Thus, in a particular case, stupidity may prevail over reason and in this case a small glimpse of reason will be sufficient to counterbalance the overpowering mass of stupidity. As in an essentially stupid man a small proof of intelligence may suddenly puzzle those who are used to regard him as absolutely stupid and incapable of a reasonable act.

Apart from the seven planets of the macrocosmos and the seven features of man, the universal gamut manifests itself in the scale of the seven colours constituting the solar spectrum as well as in the seven sounds of the musical gamut. The seven days of the week are also each under the particular domination of a double letter.

" He (God) traced them (the ' double ' letters), fashioned them, effected their combinations and their transmutations, weighed them and created by them seven stars in the world, seven days in time, seven openings (doors) in the body of man." (Ibid., IV, 5.)

These seven " doors " in the body of man by means of which he receives the impressions of the surrounding world are : " Two eyes, two ears, two nostrils, and the mouth." (Ibid., IV, 6.) These openings serve for the faculties of seeing, of hearing, of breathing (or inhaling and smelling), and for speech and the absorption of material nourishment.

It is important to know that the two letters which

correspond to a pair of parallel organs in the human head are traced in a fashion very similar one to the other. The eyes are governed by *Beth* and *Caph*; the nostrils—by *Daleth* and *Resh*; and the ears by *Phe* and *Gimel*. Each letter forming a particular pair has its individual character expressed in the tracing of the particular glyph, but is at the same time in close connection with the idea which gave form to the other letter of the pair. Thus, for example, as I have said already, the letter *Beth* represents the principle of division, or the reflection of the generating power. The letter *Caph* expresses the same idea in its second stage of development : the mould in which is formed a precise form. Numerically the former will express the number two and the latter the number twenty.

The letter *Gimel* symbolises the physical envelopment which posits the idea of formation of an organ of the human body in general and also of its physiological role. The letter *Phe* represents ideographically the mouth and the tongue, and therefore embodies the idea of the organ that emits the sound. The correspondence of the letter *Phe* with the left ear of man expresses the idea that it is by the means of this particular organ that man hears " the sound of the voice."

The signs by means of which the two nostrils are indicated are respectively *Daleth* and *Resh*. The first symbolises the idea of a material formation—the breathing which is necessary for all the manifestations of life. The letter *Resh*, according to J. Boehme, is " originated by the fiery element of nature," and therefore it expresses breathing as a process of combustion indispensable for the maintenance of heat which distinguishes a living body from a dead one.

I cannot go deeper here in the exposition of the particular influences of all these letters. The careful study of them reveals the fact that each one of the parallel organs composing a pair, though it accomplishes a mutual work forming with its companion the particular human sense—plays, nevertheless, its own part in this common work, and has its own defined and individual role.

One short example will illustrate this idea better than a long explanation. A Hindu initiate who had attained a high rank on the ladder of evolution said to me once: " You will consider that you have made the first step on the way, when you learn to control your breathing so as to *inhale with one nostril and exhale with the other.*" Try to carry this out and you will see that it is not so easy as it might seem.

I have given this example to show you the reason why the ancient initiates considered each parallel feature forming an organ of the human body, as having a particular role and being therefore governed by a particular sign, which expressed a definite application of a constructive force of nature.

The letter *Tau* which governs the mouth has in itself a double function: through the mouth the human body receives the necessary nourishment which maintains the heat of life in it. But it is also through the mouth that the Word issues forth which has the power either to create or to destroy. So the function of this letter oscillates between " this day's bread " and the Divine Verb, or in other words, between physical necessity and spiritual evolution. So the words of the Gospel: " Man shall not live by bread alone, but by every word that proceedeth out of the mouth of God " (Matt. iv, 4), find their

application in the double function of the letter *Tau*.
You remember that the word of man is the reflection
of the Divine Verb, of the Logos, by means of which
God created the world, and it is precisely this divine
faculty that distinguishes man from all the other
forms of creation and makes of him the " image of
God." I would remind the reader that the Egyptian
sign YR, which meant " to create," is formed by the
sign of the mouth combined with the one of the sun
—the symbol of light and of life.

Thus the general idea of the " double " letters of
the Hebraic alphabet expresses the individuality of
man, the choice that he makes, by his own free will,
between one quality and its opposite, or in other
words, between the way of evolution and the one of
involution. This is the reason why, in the macrocosmos, the " double " letters correspond to the
seven planets which form in the sky at the moment of
birth of man a precise combination, which will decide
his particular individuality. This combination must
not be judged from the fatalistic point of view, as it
only indicates the nature of the individual, or as the
Hindu calls it, his " Karma," showing the necessity
for struggle against certain obstacles in his way
towards the predestined evolution. It is only by the
continuous fight against the forces of evil that a man
proves his intention to attain to the good, as it is
said that " the evil tests the good." In the Egyptian
doctrine this abstract idea was expressed in the image
of the god *Shou* (personifying the force of expansion,
or of evolution) who is represented in an effort to
burst the frames opposed to his expansion by the gods
Geb and *Nut* (the personification of the force of
limitation, or in other words the involutive power).

Mathematically the number seven is composed of the three and the four, or in other words, of the principles of the ternary and the quaternary.

Thus it presents in the Hebraic symbolism the combination of the name " *IEV* " and the name " *IEVE* "—the first symbolising the creative formation in potentiality, and the second its realisation in the visible world.

The twelve " simple " letters present another formation of the above-mentioned creative powers. The twelve are disposed in four groups, each of three elements. " The twelve are ranged as if at war: three friends, three enemies; three animate, and three kill." (*Sepher Ietzirah*, VI, 5.)

In the macrocosmos, these letters correspond to the twelve signs of the Zodiac which comprise the frame in which evolve all the particular formations of the universe. This frame is stable and unchangeable as regards the relation of one element towards another.

The mutual relations of the Zodiacal signs are established once and for ever, and their movement constitutes the general revolving movement of the circle, each sign occupying in it its own established place. Thus the astrological influence which a particular sign exercises on an individual or on an event will depend on the hour, as the apparent revolution of the Zodiacal circle is completed in twenty-four hours. The particular place occupied by a sign in a given hour (either on one of the points of the horizon, or in the Zenith, or in the Nadir, etc.) will determine the precise influence which this sign emanates at that moment. The combination of the planets, which influences the formation of the moment, will inscribe itself in the frame of the Zodiacal circle and will receive the particular tint (one may be allowed the expression) of the Zodiacal signs in which the combinations are formed.

In the human body the twelve " simple " letters govern the functions of the body (the digestion, the current of blood, the lymphatic system, etc.), which are under the control of the so-called " subconscious forces " of the human soul. The reason of man does not control these natural functions, and man can neither stop nor accelerate the processes which are carried out in his body automatically.

This is the reason why these letters are called " simple," as they do not possess the double nature (the quality and the defect which characterise the double letters), and therefore do not necessitate the choice by man of the way to take.

The forces emanated by these letters rule the vegetable and animal life of nature and therefore are purely and solely involutive. Their influence stops at the maximum of division of the primordial unity— the *eight*, and thus they concern in man the work of his body, or in other terms, of the animal part of his being.

" He (God) traced, fashioned them (the twelve simple letters), made their combinations and their transpositions, weighed them and created by them the twelve signs of Zodiac in the world, twelve months in the year, twelve guides (chiefs) in the body of man. . . ." (*Sepher Ietzirah*, V, 3.)

It is important to remember that, as I have stated, all these letters constitute *the frame* in which evolves the life of the universe. Thus, though their influence is clearly felt in all the different manifestations of the creation, they cannot be considered either good or evil.   They are like the different forces of nature (water, fire, electricity, etc.) which can be directed by man either towards a good end and participate in construction, or towards a bad end and then exert their destructive power.

I will come back to the question of the universal gamut and of the twelve forces forming the natural frame, when I expound the ancient science called Astrology, as it will then be necessary to study the different influences combined in a particular formation which decides the individuality of a human being, or determines a particular event.

The whole world is like a perfect and complicated machine, like a clock-work, in which the movement of one wheel produces the movement of another. Every part of the machinery accomplishes its particular work, and all of them taken together constitute the life of the universe.   Man is only a small wheel in this great machine and therefore his life is submitted to the general laws.   But apart from that, man being created in the image of God, possesses a part of the Divine Reason and a free will which allow him to choose the way of evolution.   Thus, though he is subject to the general working of the universal machinery, at the same time he can orient his own acts either towards spirituality, or bury his spiritual part in matter.   This individual work of man will be reflected in the work of the whole universe.   The destination of man is to bring the universe to the state of perfection, or in other words, to accomplish the cycle in transforming the involutive power into the evolutive power.   The creation that preceded man was produced by consecutive divisions of the primordial Unity, and thus it was carried out by analysis. The destination of man is to synthesise the innumerable particles which animate the different forms of creation, and to bring them back to the Principle from which they emanated.

Thus though Man by his nature was a product of the maximum of penetration of the involutive force of division, by his reason (*Aish*), the particle of God, he conceives the synthetic power of evolution, which he must put into action by means of his free will, his companion, his spiritual wife (*Aisha*).

This idea was rendered in the Egyptian teaching by the myth depicting the struggle between *Horus* (the perfect man—Adam) and *Seth*—the personification of the involutive power. This struggle ended in the victory of Horus who "joined the two lands" together and became their sole ruler. Thus this legend gives an idea of the predestined victory of man, over the coagulating power of involution, a victory which will bring the world to its state of perfection, to the Principle from which it emanated. In the Bible this same idea is expressed in the promise that " the seed of the woman shall bruise the head of the serpent."

CHAPTER IV

THE SEPHIROTHIC SYSTEM

"GOD has created His Universe by the three Sepharim: Sepher, Sephor, and Sepour." (*Sepher Ietzirah*, I, 1.) With these mysterious words begins the book of Creation, named the *Sepher Ietzirah*. The meaning of the word "*Sepharim*" can be rendered literally by "numeration," or "reckoning." The three words: *Sepher*, *Sephor*, and *Sepour* are composed identically of the three same consonants: *Sameh*, *Phe*, and *Resh*. The vowels which differentiate these three words are rendered, according to the rule of the Hebraic writing (which is the same as that of Arabic), by particular pointing. These words mean respectively: "reckoning," "book," and "account of numbers." Aberdanès translates these words: *writing, reckoning,* and *verb*; another Cabalist, Troubitch, by *reckoning, speech,* and *writing*. The Divine word is simultaneously His "Writing," the Divine thought is His "Word"; thus the thought, the word, and the writing of God are not three different things as they are with man, but one and only one.

As I already indicated, the Sephiroths of the Hebraic Cabala represent simultaneously the decimal system and the mysterious "Attributes" of God, which penetrate into the depths of Creation. These two qualities, which at first sight do not seem to have anything in common, are nevertheless closely conjoined and complete one another when one seeks to comprehend the essence of the Cosmogony. The ten numbers explained the symbolic idea of creation in six days, as well as the role of man, the culminating point of definite development which crowned the marvellous work of God. The ten "Attributes" gave birth to the Ten Commandments, forming thus the frame in which must evolve the life of man in his progress on the ladder of evolution. The ten numbers constitute the mathematics and the mechanics of the universe; they symbolise the fabric on which is embroidered the design realised by means of the "Attributes." These two particulars of the Sephiroths joined together reveal a complete and admirable picture of the life of the Cosmos.

Let us try to throw some light on what has been said.

The Ten Sephiroths are formed of three distinct groups which are closely bound together. The first group presents the three superior Sephiroths : *Kether*, *Chochma*, and *Binah*, which symbolise the first manifestation (the ternary) of the divine principle. As you know, the idea of the ternary is at the base of all developed religions and in the Christian religion is expressed by the Holy Trinity.

God, the Unknown, the Omnipotent, the " Ain Soph " of the Hebraic Cabala, " Tem " of the ancient Egyptian teaching—cannot be conceived by the intelligence of man. In the book of Genesis it is stated in allegorical terms, that man after having committed the original sin had hidden himself, as he could no more contemplate the face of God. Man having fallen into the depths of matter can no more

L

see nor understand the " Absolute." Thus God, who is the Supreme Wisdom Itself, makes Himself felt through the Omniscient Reason emanated from the Crown *Kether*, which dominates all creation.

The Sephirothic " Attributes " govern the world by imposing on it their immanent laws, and the first and basic law is that of equilibrium, or in other words, the one expressed by the ternary. Thus the number three is at the summit of the divine work. This number symbolises the first division that creates life (the Egyptian *Mout-F*), the positive and negative poles of the magnet with its neutral point ; it is the union of man and woman ; it is, in fine, the fundamental law of equilibrium which is at the starting-point of creation.

The three first Commandments of the Decalogue concerning the worship of God correspond to the ternary, and therefore to the three first Sephiroths. They establish the principle of God, being the One and Only Cause which emanated from Himself all the creation. The second Commandment states that nothing among the things created can replace or represent God. The third Commandment forbids man to evoke the name of God in vain. (Exod. xx, 1, 7.)

These three Commandments, which constitute the basis of religion, correspond naturally to the three Sephiroths, expressing the principles of the whole creation.

The second group of the Sephirothic system is formed of six elements called the " Constructive Sephiroths." They answer to the six symbolic days of creation which present a realisation in the visible world of the principle enounced by the first ternary. This group can be itself divided into two secondary

subdivisions, forming each, according to the fundamental law, a separate and equilibrated ternary. The
essential difference between these secondary ternaries
and their prototype consists in the fact that in the
primordial ternary *the equilibrium is in the principle*, in
the unity itself (the Balance that was in the Ancient
of Days), and that the two poles in which the unity
divided itself are born in a perfect state of equilibrium.
All the following ternaries, and in particular the ones
constituting the second group of the Sephirothic
system, symbolised a particular form of realisation,
and their equilibrium results from the shock of two
opposing forces. Thus the equilibrium is no more the
reason, as in the prototype, but the *effect* of the establishment of particular mutual relations of two opposing
forces.

Graphically the Supreme ternary is usually represented by a triangle with the summit oriented upwards,
to express the idea that it emanates from the primordial
Unity and that its point of equilibrium resides in the
Unity itself.

The secondary ternaries are, on the contrary,
pictured by a triangle inverted, that is to say, having
the summit pointing downwards. This expresses the
idea that the equilibrium in a particular ternary is
obtained as a result of the shock of two opposing
forces. Thus the second group of the Sephirothic
system is usually represented by two triangles having
their summits downwards.

The first Sephirah of the second group is called
Chezed, and it corresponds to the fourth Commandment, which says, that the work must be done during
six days and that the seventh day is consecrated to rest.
Thus it outlines the idea of all the six " Sephiroths of

Construction " by which was accomplished the creative work in the six symbolic days. I will explain later the meaning of the seventh day—the day of rest.

The next Sephirahs of Construction defined the different phases of the work of God, and in regard to man it shows the sins, or, using the terminology of ancient teaching, " the bark," from which the spirit of man must liberate itself in order to merit the predestined recompense—the rest after labour, the struggle of life, which the spirit that has accomplished its destiny gains.

The fourth and the fifth Sephirahs (*Chezed* and *Geburah*) are equilibrated by the sixth, named *Tiphereth*, forming thus the first triangle of reflection, the one that constitutes the first part of the six " Constructive Sephiroths."

In the creation, *Chezed* symbolises the appearance of light, which is considered as the first manifestation of life, the first form of vibration which awoke the passivity, the first movement which animated the inert mass of primal matter. In the Egyptian teaching this idea was expressed in the appearance of the God *Shou*, the one who simultaneously personified the idea of light and of air—both essential elements for life on earth.

But to light is opposed darkness, as the force of limitation is opposed to that of expansion, and involution to evolution, in order to constitute the necessary equilibrium (or ternary in the image of the one of prototype). The coagulating power was personified in the Egyptian pantheon by the goddess *Tefnut*, the companion of *Shou*. The Bible expresses the same idea in the words : " And God divided the light from the darkness." (Gen. i, 4.)

The second day of creation corresponds to the Sephirah *Geburah*. This day is that in which was established the idea of space, or in other words, were posed the material boundaries in which would evolve all future manifestations of life. " And God said : let there be a firmament in the midst of the water and let it divide the waters from the waters. And God made the firmament and divided the waters which were under the firmament from the waters which were above the firmament." (Gen. i, 6, 7.) Here we see a slight difference between the rendering of the same idea, by Moses, and by the Egyptian doctrine. According to the latter the second couple emanated from *Ra*, which constituted the actual limitation and was personified by the god *Geb* (the earth) and the goddess *Nut* (the sky, the firmament). In the Egyptian teaching the waters represented the primal matter, the element out of which were created all the following physical elements. Thus by the name of the god of the earth, *Geb*, the Egyptians intended *all the world below* : the earth as well as the seas—everything which is defined by Moses as the " waters below."

The Bible specifies the separation of the waters and the dry land, which was performed on the third day. But according to the Bible the earth created by this last separation of elements was already provided with vegetative power and brought forth grass and fruit trees.

According to the Egyptian teaching this idea was symbolised in the appearance of the third couple, *Osiris-Isis*, that personified the generating power and the mother earth.

In the Sephirothic system, after the two first Sephirahs of the constructive group, follows the third, named *Tiphereth* ; that equilibrates the first triangle of manifestation. It symbolises the first realisation of movement in space—the separation of elements which produces necessarily as a consequence the first manifestation of life—the vegetative power. It can be therefore personified by the grain or the fruit " whose seed was in itself after its kind."

The following manifestation of the generating power is pursued in the consecutive division of the cell into two, four, eight, etc., and this division constitutes the mystery of life developing from death and necessitating the burial of the grain and its " joining to the earth," or in metaphoric language : the union of Osiris and Isis.

Thus the Sephirah *Tiphereth* reigns over the division or individualisation of the principle of life which manifests itself in the birth of different species of plants, each of them bearing seed " after its kind." But this process is not yet complete as *things are different only in their particular kind and not individually.* The penetration of the principle of life must as yet pass through different phases of animal life to arrive at its ultimate point, to the complete individual— man possessing his own free will.

From another point of view and according to the teaching of the Cabalists, *Tiphereth* signifies *Beauty* or *Harmony*, which constitutes the base of the triangle *Chezed—Geburah—Tiphereth*. At the same time this Sephirah is the centre of the whole system, and thus represents the ideal, around which is constructed the whole of the divine work of creation.

In the creative cycle, *Nezach*, the seventh Sephirah, corresponds to the creation of stars. This might at first seem strange, and we can remark that here the teaching of the Cabala differs from that given in the Egyptian initiation schools. But from what follows you will understand that the idea of the creators of the Cabalistic system is logical and that this correspondence of the seventh Sephirah is quite appropriate.

You remember that the translation of the Bible which is known under the name of Vulgate does not render the symbolic meaning of the original text, which contained in a hidden form the essence of the teaching of Moses. The first word with which the book of Genesis begins is rendered in the ordinary translation by the words " In the beginning." This translation does not express the idea which the writer of the book of Genesis wanted to convey to one who was advanced enough to understand him. In the Greek translation the same word is rendered by a more appropriate expression : " *En Arche*," meaning *In principle*. This throws a different light upon all that follows this first word, suggesting the idea that previously the world was not created in its material state as one might conclude from the translation of the Vulgate, but " in principle," or otherwise " in potentiality."

Thus, in order to realise the individualisation of life on earth, the Creator had to constitute a material centre out of which all the formations could draw the necessary vital forces. This centre, which emanates out of itself simultaneously, the light and the vivifying power, is the sun, the role of which is known to everyone. The importance of this luminary was evident to all ancient people and therefore they worshipped it as the principal god of their pantheon. The Egyptians in particular had put the god " Ra " at the head of the Ennead of creation and appropriated to him the role of centre of light as well as the expression of the divine word which ordered all creation.

The influence of the different planets on life on earth, studied since the most remote times, constituted the science called Astrology. Man, observing the rhythmic revolution of the stars, established the division of time, which is not accidental, but based upon the mechanism of celestial phenomena. We find in the book of Genesis confirmation of this idea as we read in the correct interpretation, that the stars, apart from their role of torches of physical light, were also created to " enlighten the intelligence of man." This statement is very important, as it is precisely by observing the stars of the sky in their constant movement that man could start his investigations of the mechanism of the universe. These observations forced his intelligence to elevate itself from the earth and gave him the first idea that life was not limited to the surface of the earth. Observation of the stars opened the eyes of man and enlarged his mental horizon, developing in him his spiritual part and directing him on the way of progress and of evolution traced for him by the Creator.

Thus we see that the moment of creation of the luminaries and stars is well attributed to the Sephirah *Nezach*, which signifies " *Movement.*"

The divine work is continued and developed in the following stage of individualisation of the generative power by the formation of the first living beings—the fishes and the birds. To this moment corresponds the eighth Sephirah, *Hod*, which means stabilisation, " calmness."

As you see, the meaning of this Sephirah is opposed to that of the previous one. If *Nezach* expresses the turbulent movement of creative forces in full action, *Hod* represents the calmness, the passiveness, the opposition which puts a brake on the movement and which forces the disturbed elements to take a precise shape and to maintain it.

Thus, coming back to the Egyptian teaching, we can say that the Sephirah *Nezach* expresses the action of the principle of expansion personified by the god *Shou*, and the Sephirah *Hod* corresponds to the action of the principle of limitation personified by the goddess *Tefnut*. But as these two principles have attained the state of deep inter-penetration (expressed by the number eight)—the first Sephirah (*Nezach*) will correspond to the realisation of the active, or evolutive principle personified by *Osiris* (the vivifying power); and *Hod* will correspond to the coagulating and materialising force personified by the god *Seth* (the brick).

The last Sephirah of the second group, which terminates the so-called " Constructive Sephiroths " —is *Iezod*. It is called the " *Foundation,*" as it presents the point of equilibrium of the triangle *Nezach—Hod—Iezod*, and also the point whereat is summed up the whole edifice of the constructive forces.

As *Kether* is the principle of equilibrium which orients the whole system, *Iezod* is its manifestation in full expansion, and therefore it presents the foundation of the whole edifice.

In regard to the days of creation *Iezod* is the sixth day, that in which the individualisation of the principle of life attained to its maximum in the creation of the diverse species of animals, and at last the moment came when man appeared, as the crowning stone of the edifice of creation.

Iezod is the sixth Constructive Sephirah, and in the general order of the whole system presents the number *nine*—the one that characterises Adam, the universal man.

The work of the Creator was completed definitely in the sixth day by the creation of man, the culminating point, the end, the number nine. Thus in the ninth Sephirah the Divine principle penetrated to the bottom of the creation and the division of the Unity attained its maximum. Man is the being in whom the analytic penetration is now fully developed and begins the synthetic ascension back to the primordial Unity.

The real sense of life is expressed under the form of the Sephirothic system in its gradual development from one to nine and from nine back to one. Man is placed at the culminating point of the maximum of division, and his role is to reduce this division of manifestation to the principle of Unity. This is the reason why the place of man is naturally in the Sephirah *Iezod*—the culminating point of the creative manifestation, the base of all the system, the end of the cycle of involution, after which must begin that of evolution. Man was created " in the image of God "; thus, according to the Egyptian definition, he possesses the knowledge of the " two greatnesses " : the one of synthetic unity and the one of analytic unity. He possesses *reason* (*Aish*) which is a particle, a spark of the Centre of Light represented by *Kether* in its deepest penetration to the bottom of creation. In order to direct his evolution on the precipitous way of elevation, God provided this reason with a companion, *free will* (*Aisha*), which puts into action the conceptions of the reason. This synthetic work which man must accomplish is rendered in the

PLATE VII

COMPARATIVE TABLE OF THE SEPHIROTHIC SYSTEM WITH THE EGYPTIAN ENNEAD.

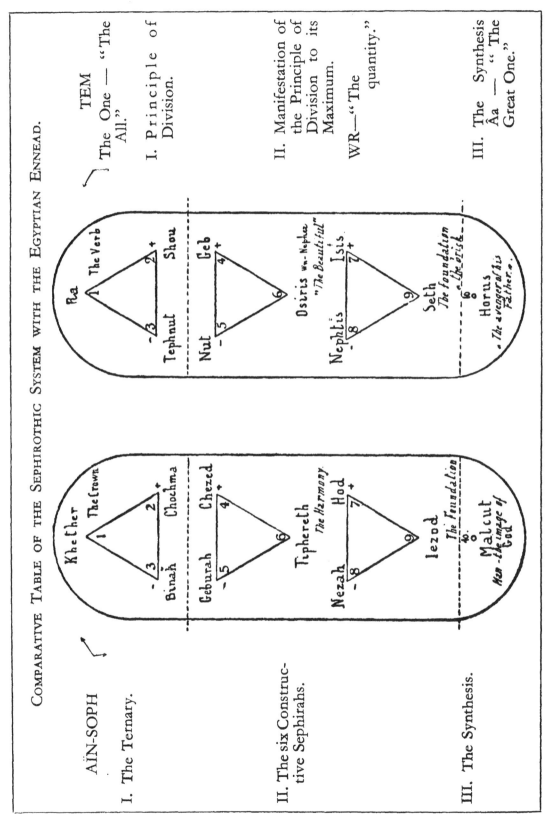

Sephirothic system in the tenth Sephirah, *Malcuth*—ten, the unity of second degree, or in other words, the realisation, the sum reducing the whole system to its primitive state.

Thus *Malcuth* corresponds in the creation to the *seventh* day—the one of rest, the end of the cycle which sums up the whole work, and after which begins a new cycle.

In the Cabala it is " Ain Soph "—the Ancient of Days—who is at the top, at the start; and it is *Malcuth* who is at the bottom, at the end, in which we catch a glimpse of a new beginning. In the Egyptian teaching the first corresponds to *Tem*—the cause of life, the " All " in the state of *potentiality*. The second corresponds to *Horus*, the child, the result, the " All " in the state of *realisation*. " That which is above is as that which is below," as stated by the medieval thinkers, and all is in Unity and Unity itself. Thus you will understand the statement in the book of Creation which says : " Ten immaterial (abstract) numbers (Sephiroths), ten, and *not* nine ; ten, and *not* eleven ; understand by your sense of comprehension and conceive by your sense of understanding ; put them to the test, scrutinise them, establish them each as it is necessary, and place the Creator at His place. . . . Ten immaterial numbers (Sephiroths), their end is in the potentiality of being in their beginning, like the flame which is in potentiality in the coal. As God is alone and there does not exist a second, what number can you name (which would be) before One." (*Sepher Ietzirah*, XI, 4, 7.)

These words sum up all the ideas expressed by the whole Sephirothic system. The ten numbers of the decimal numeration which present the external form of the Sephiroths render their philosophic concepts in a precise and tangible form. This wonderful system contains in itself all the laws that rule the life of the Universe and guide the progress of man. One cannot add an element to it as one can neither substract from it an element without deranging the idea which informs the whole system; as it is said, that they are " ten, and not nine ; ten, and not eleven." They contain in the form of the first three Sephirahs the basic principle of the ternary, the six Constructive Sephirahs express the realisation of this principle in its penetration of the material world.

The same six Constructive Sephiroths, with the last one, *Malcuth*, form the universal gamut by means of which the law of equilibrium governs all the manifestations of the visible world. The only element that does not enter into the Sephirothic system is the duodenary, the Zodiacal circle. This is quite comprehensible; the Sephirothic system is one which expresses the idea of the individual's evolution, the work of the two opposed currents which in the individual are equilibrated one in regard to the other. Thus the dominant idea of this system is one that concerns life in its continuous changes and the struggle of the two opposing forces. The duodenary expresses on the contrary the laws which were established once and for ever in an unchangeable order to create a frame in which would evolve the life of the universe. Therefore the idea of the duodenary could not be included in the Sephirothic system, as the latter is purely dynamic and the first is static.

As I have said already, the ten Sephiroths enter into the system of the Hebraic alphabet as they correspond to the first ten letters of it, but at the same time they are distinctly different from the twenty-two letters and constitute with these last the sum of *thirty-two*, called by the Cabalists " the thirty-two ways of wisdom." This system is based upon the words with which the book of Creation begins and which states that the world was created " by thirty-two ways, beautiful and full of wisdom."

I hope that this short exposition of one of the most difficult problems of the Hebraic Cabala will enable the reader to understand, certainly not the essence, but at all events, the general scheme comprised by the ancient thought. Deeper penetration into the subject necessitates long and arduous study.

CHAPTER V

THE SYSTEMS

IN continuation of the foregoing sketch of the principal laws, expressed by means of the twenty-two letters of the Hebraic alphabet, I will proceed to a consideration on general lines of the different systems that were invented by the Cabalists in order to apply the laws of nature to life in its diverse phases. But I must first explain what is to be understood by the term " Cabala."

This word can be written either as *Caph-Beth-Lamed*, or *Coph-Beth-Lamed*. In the first case it meant " chain," and in the second " tradition." It will be seen that these two alternatives are practically synonymous. What does the word " tradition " mean ? It is the chain that joins the initiator to his disciple, the chain by means of which the former transmits his knowledge to the latter. This chain reaches back to the remotest times, when writing did not exist, or if it existed, it was not considered safe to entrust to it the greatest secrets of nature.

Thus the primitive tradition was purely oral, and therefore the meaning of the word Cabala is also " what is passed from hand to hand." As the Cabala constituted the secret knowledge enveloped in complicated cryptographic systems, this word in the course of time and in European languages received the meaning of " something mysterious," hidden, or of something complicated and obscure. In French we meet with the expression: *cabbale de théâtre*, which was used to denote a secret organisation imposing its will with a view to creating the success of an actor, or of a play, or on the contrary to make a scandal in the theatre in order to spoil a production.

In the course of time the oral tradition had to be written in some way in order that it should not be lost altogether, or completely degraded. But as it was considered that the secrets constituting the Cabala could not be revealed to an unprepared mind, different enigmatic devices were invented in which allegories, metaphors and all sorts of transpositions were used in order to hide the secret knowledge from the profane.

Thus there appeared different Cabalistic systems, each having its own key, by means of which the adept could unravel the skein in which the real meaning was entangled.

Most of these systems are based upon the transposition of letters. We find the idea of this device expressed in the following verse of the book of Creation: " How did He (God) trace them and how did He perform (the combinations and the transmutations)? One letter with all and all the letters with one, two letters with all and all the letters with two, etc. . . ." (*Sepher Ietzirah*, II, 5.)

This text gave the idea of constituting the so-called mathematical systems of transmutation which received the name of tables of Ziruf from the word *Zirufim*— to transpose.

The theoretical part of the Cabala is contained in two books: *Sepher Ietzirah*, or the " Book of Creation," and *Sepher Ha Zohar*, or the " Celestial Chariot."

The practical part is expounded in the " *Notarikon*," in the " *Temourah*," and in the " *Gematria*," all together forming the *Talmud*. Many of the methods which we study in these books belong to the domain of cryptography.

The *Notarikon* is based upon the consideration that every letter entering into a word can be taken as an initial letter forming a new word. Thus the primitive word gives birth to certain new words, the study of which will contribute a further explanation of the word that generated them. Apart from this, every letter having its particular interpretation, one could develop the last according to the letters entering into the composition of the name or word forming the subject of study. In order that this statement may be fully understood it is necessary to give an example of the above-mentioned procedure.

David, in the testament to his son Solomon, says : " He cursed me with cruel maledictions," which in Hebrew is expressed in the word *Nimrezet*. According to the general rule of the ancient Hebraic language, a word was expressed only by the consonants, the vowels not being written but only supposed. Thus, the word that interests us will read " *NMRZT*," which means " He called me." To know to what maledictions David alludes, every one of these letters is taken and considered as an initial letter of a word, obtaining thus the following curses : *N-oef*—adulterer, *M-ohabi*—mohabit (which was an offence to David, who was the son of Ruth), *R-ozeah*—murderer, *Z-orer*—horrible, *T-ohera*—abject.

The other system, called " *Temourah*," is based upon the different transpositions of letters entering into a word, creating thus new words, the analysis of which

M

reveals the mysterious meaning of the original word. It is precisely this system which is at the base of the so-called "tables of Ziruf."

This is an example of the methods used by the *Temourah*. The word with which the book of Genesis begins is in Hebrew *Barashit*, translated "in the beginning," or "in principle." This word can be divided into two words: *Bara*, meaning "He said," or "He created," and *Shit*, meaning "six." Thus, in the first words of his book, Moses defines that the Creation was accomplished in six days or in six periods. This is a simple decomposition of a word, but one could also make a transposition of letters forming the same word. For example, one read: *Bara-ish*, which means "He created the *Ish*," or the primal matter, the first substance out of which were formed by differentiation all the manifestations of the visible World. The *Ish* corresponds to the Egyptian god *Nou*, the one who personified the primal matter as well as the forces of nature in a latent state. As you remember, *Nou*, according to the Egyptian teaching, was created in the beginning by the active word of God.

Here is another example of transmutation of letters taught by the *Temourah*.

In the book of Exodus, God says: "I will send before you my angel." This last word was written *Malechi*. In transposing the letters that formed this word, one obtains the name *Michael*, which is the name of the angel who was considered the protector of the Hebrew nation.

Lastly, the book called "*Gematria*" expounds the purely mathematical systems based upon a knowledge of the Sephiroths and upon all sorts of transpositions and other manipulations with the letters composing a name which are considered in their numeric meaning.

The tables " *Ziruf* " are related to this system. They are composed in a few different fashions. The simplest, called the " Rational table," was constructed thus : one wrote all the twenty-two letters of the alphabet from right to left in their natural order, beginning by the letter *Aleph* and finishing by *Tau*. Then the same was done from the letter *Aleph* downward, thus one obtained two lines starting from the letter *Aleph* and forming a right angle, the two ends of which both presented the twenty-second letter of the alphabet—*Tau*. This right angle constituted two sides of a square composed of lines of twenty-two letters each beginning from the top or from the right by the letter of the original line that formed the right angle, and containing all the twenty-two letters of the alphabet in their natural order. Thus the second line began by the letter *Beth* and finished by *Aleph*, the third by the letter *Gimel* and finished by *Beth*, and so on. If one wanted to find a key for understanding the hidden meaning of a root composed of two letters, one took the first letter composing this root in the horizontal line forming the framing of the square and the second letter in the vertical line forming with the first a right angle. The intersection of these two lines in the square gave the necessary letter which served as key for the given root.

This simplest table was developed in a number of other tables called " irregular," in which the order of letters was either transposed altogether (for example, from left to right), or the letters in a line were submitted to a transmutation according to some elaborated system. Then come the so-called *double*, or combined

tables, "*Ziruf*," in which every square is occupied by
two letters, forming a root. Thus the first letter
would enter in all the squares of the first vertical rank
combined successfully with every one of the other
letters of the alphabet. In the next rank would come
other combinations of two letters based upon the
formation of the primitive line and so on till the end.
All the possible combinations of two letters entered
thus in the table and one precise combination could
enter only once and was never repeated. One
obtained by the means of this table (proceeding in the
same way as was explained for the first regular table)
—a new root which revealed the mysterious meaning
of the roots that one submitted to the study by the
Ziruf table. You understand that one can form a
great number of tables of the same kind, each of
which is based upon a particular combination of
letters.

Another system evolved from the Gematria is that
of the so-called "*Magic squares*." These squares were
attributed each to a different planet which defined
the respective number of cells forming the square.
Thus the square of Saturn was formed of *nine* cells
(three composing each side of it), the one of Jupiter
—of *sixteen* cells formed in lines of four, the one of
Mars presented *twenty-five* cells (5×5) and so on. In
each square was written a letter which was considered
in its numeric meaning. The sum of the numbers
formed either by a vertical or a horizontal line of the
given square presented a constant number the same
for all the lines which would constitute the precise
square.

Mathematically it is easy to construct a square
answering to this condition ; for example, for a square

of twenty-five cells one has got fifty different combinations from which to obtain the necessary result. But all these mathematical squares were not considered as *Magic* squares. There could exist *only one* combination which was considered as a Magic square, and this combination was defined by a particular scheme, which accompanied the square and by applying which one obtained the necessary combination called *Magic*. This scheme indicated the transpositions which had to be made in order to obtain the necessary disposition of numbers. Once the precise square was constituted, there existed another scheme by means of which one obtained from the square answers to questions to be resolved. We find the representation of these " magical squares " in many works treating of the question of magic. They are all based upon the work of a medieval writer, Cornelius Aggrippa, who gives in his book, *The Occult Philosophy of Magic*, the representation of all these squares with their schemes of compositions, but he leaves the understanding of their application to the reader. The authors who followed Agrippa simply copied this part of his work, not giving any explanations, perhaps because they did not understand themselves how this system had to be used.

The simplest application of the Gematria is given in the so-called *Ain Bekar*, or system of nine squares. This system was composed by the formation of nine squares in each of which were disposed three letters, thus, in the first square (counting from the right) the letters: *Aleph, Iod*, and *Coph*, giving respectively the numbers 1, 10, and 100. In the second square were disposed the letters: *Beth, Caph*, and *Resh*, presenting the numbers 2, 20, and 200, and so on. In order to constitute the numbers from 500

to 900 the Hebraic alphabet used the so-called
"terminal letters" which differed slightly by their
glyph from the original letter. Thus, for example, the
letter *Noun* expressed the number 50, and the terminal
Noun the number 500; the letter *Sameh* presented the
number 60 and the terminal *Sameh*—600, and so on.

The system *Ain Bekar* gave the idea of constituting
the symbolic writing which was employed, for
example, to form the so-called "seals of archangels."

Yet another system of the Cabala is the so-called
Shemamphorash, or the "name of seventy-two letters."
This system is based upon the principle of transposition as well as on the one of mathematics given
by the Gematria. The idea of this system is given in
the text of the Scriptures where it is said: "My
angel will go before you, look at him, as he bears
My great Name," this is to say the name of seventy-two
letters.

To compose the *Shemamphorash* the Cabalists took
from the fourteenth chapter of the book of Exodus
the verses 19, 20, and 21, each composed of *seventy-two
letters*, and beginning respectively by the words:
Vaiysa, *Vaiaba*, and *Vaiet*.

These verses were written one under the other so
that in the first and last verse the letters were disposed
from left to right and in the second verse—from right
to left. Thus were composed seventy-two names
each of three letters. Then to each of the names so
obtained was added the termination either *IAH* or
EL, which are themselves names of God. Each of
the seventy-two names of the *Shemamphorash* presents
a particular formation and a precise combination of
constructive forces of creation. In a remarkable work
called *The Cabalistic Science*, Lenain gives a detailed

study of the system of *Shemamphorash*. This system can be used in application to Cabalistic astrology, and helps to resolve many problems.

The scheme presenting the disposition of seventy-two names round the Zodiacal circle gives, for example, a wonderful idea of the formation of the electric current in a dynamo. The name Tetragrammaton revolving in the centre constitutes by its letters the positive and negative poles of the anchor, and the seventy-two names disposed on the external rim of the circle constitute the enrolling of the wire in which is formed the secondary magnetic current.

There are many other possible applications of this wonderful system, which would necessitate too long an explanation to be considered in this chapter.

· Another system of the same kind is expressed in the so-called *Rota*, or " wheel of creation." This also is based upon the revolution of the name *Ieve* round a centre which produces twelve transpositions of the letters entering in its formation. These twelve new names are projected in the periphery constituted by the twelve signs of the Zodiac, disposed in such order as to form a frame surrounding the centre. The combination of letters of the sacred name with those corresponding to the signs of the Zodiac and planets (which occupy in a horoscope a place in a precise sign)—indicates the particular influences which an individual receives at his birth. In order to apply the *Rota* to a particular individual the letters of the sacred name were replaced by the corresponding letters composing the name of the individual. I will return to a consideration of the *Rota* when I examine the theory of Astrology.

The study and application of the different Cabalistic

systems might seem childish play, but, as says Eliphas Levy : " It is as difficult as the most difficult problem."

Apart from the mathematical systems I have mentioned, there existed other purely philosophic combinations. The two following systems, that of the " thirty-two ways of wisdom " and that of the " fifty gates of reason," belong to this second group.

I have already explained the idea of the so-called " thirty-two ways " which are formed mathematically by the addition of the ten Sephiroths to the twenty-two letters of the alphabet. It is interesting to note here that the Cabalists who based their theories on the books of Moses have remarked that in the first chapter of the book of Genesis the name " Aeloim," by which is defined the Creator (" He—the—gods ") in the act of emanating from Himself the creative powers, is repeated *thirty-two* times. Refer also to the text of the book of Creation in which is stated the way by which the creative power manifested itself. " Two stones build two houses, three stones build six houses, four stones build twenty-four houses." (*Sepher Ietzirah*, IV, 15.) This text defines the rules of transpositions of letters according to the system of *Ziruf*, two letters giving two different transpositions, three giving six, four—twenty-four, and so on.

Thus the *analytic system* of the *Sepher Ietzirah* starts from the idea of God which it develops in the creation by using the combinations of letters. It is called by the Cabalists the system of " thirty-two ways of wisdom." To this system is opposed another, purely *deductive*, which departs from the observation of the phenomena of nature to arrive at the comprehension of God. This system is called the one of

" fifty gates of reason." The first system is, as you understand, based upon faith and presents the religious aspect, expressing the penetration of the divine power into the depths of matter—the *involutive* movement.

The second is based upon the observations by man of natural phenomena and therefore presents the scientific outlook. It expresses the *evolutive* movement of the reason of man who sees in the slightest manifestation of nature the presence of the creative power of God. These two systems complete one another, and together they define the point of view of the ancients who combined the sage with the priest. According to the statement of the Cabala, each of these two systems is derived from one of the supreme Sephiroths forming the base of the first triangle. The system of " thirty-two ways " is evolved from the Sephirah *Chochma*, and the one of " fifty gates " from the Sephirah *Binah*. According to Khircher none can start on the " ways of wisdom " before having passed through the " gates of reason."

Each of these two systems completes the other, and this is clearly shown in their mathematic composition. Each of them presents, following the rule of reduction to the primitive numbers—the number *five* ($50=5$, $32=3+2=5$).

Thus each of them presents the half of the complete cycle which is *ten*. This idea is clearly stated in the book of Creation in the following terms: " Ten immaterial (abstract) numbers (Sephiroths) according to the number of the ten fingers—*five against five*— but the alliance of unity is between them." (*Sepher Ietzirah*, I, 3.)

The evolutive system of the " fifty gates " is composed of six groups. *The first group* formed of ten particular gates expounds the principle of elements of nature beginning (first gate) with the primal matter, or the *Ysh*, according to the denomination of the Cabalists. The ninth and tenth gates express respectively the principles of differentiation of elements and their mutation, or mixing, in order to constitute a precise form of physical existence.

The second group analyses these mutations (or mixtures) and is also composed of ten elements. The first element of this group studies the differentiation of minerals obtained by the division of the principle, and is under the reign of the letter *Caph*. The last element of this group concerns the Creation of animal life, " the living soul," according to the definition of the book of Genesis. It is under the rule of the letter *Shin*, and corresponds to the beginning of the sixth day of creation—the appearance on earth of different species of animals which preceded the creation of man.

The third group treats of the human decade and is also composed of ten elements. The first element of this group concerns the creation of universal man—Adam, and is under the domination of the letter *Tau*. This group presents in its ten elements the development of the creative idea of God which combined the complex being of man out of three distinct elements : the body taken from the earth, the soul developed by the animal, and the spiritul part, " the breath of God," which sets man apart from and over all other forms of creation. Thus the last element of this group will present man as a perfected being, the image of God ; and will correspond to the end of the sixth day of creation, the ultimate manifestation of the creative power.

PLATE VIII

RATIONAL TABLE ZIRUF

		6	5	4	3	2	1
22 7		6	5	4	3	2	1
1 8		7	6	5	4	3	2
2 9		8	7	6	5	4	3
3 10		9	8	7	6	5	4
4 11		10	9	8	7	6	5
5 12		11	10	9	8	7	6
		12	11	10	9	8	7
		⋮	⋮	⋮	⋮	⋮	⋮
			2	1	22		
			3	2	1	22	
		5	4	3	2	1	22

Example : The key for the root composed of the 6 and 7 letters will be the 12th letter.

MAGIC SQUARE OF JUPITER

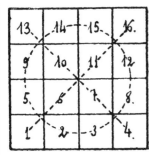

1. Manipulation.

Scheme of
Transpositions.

4	14	15	1
9	7	6	12
5	11	10	8
16	2	3	13

2. Result.

AIN BEKAR TABLE

300	30	3	200	20	2	100	10	1
...	..	.	...	..	.	...	..	.
ש	ל	ג	ר	כ	ב	ק	י	א
600	60	6	500	50	5	400	40	4
...	..	.	...	..	.	...	..	.
ס	נ	ו	ן	נ	ה	ת	מ	ד
900	90	9	800	80	8	700	70	7
...	..	.	...	..	.	...	..	.
ץ	צ	ט	ף	פ	ח	ן	ע	ז

Example : Michaël.

מיכאל

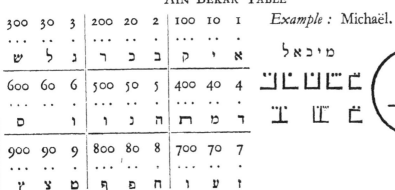

The fourth group expounds the order of development of the heavens in regard to the earth and man. It begins therefore by the formation of the spheres, then come the seven planets in reverse order to that given in the book of Creation (as here the formation of these elements is considered from below, from the point of view of man, and not from the point of view of consecutive division of the principle). The last element of this group concerns the empiric world, the "Temple of God," and is under the domination of the letter *Iod*.

The fifth group treats of the world of the superior forces of creation, or in other words, of the "nine dignities of angels." Thus it is composed of nine elements beginning with the *Cherubim* and ending with the *Chaiot Chakodesh* or the "sacred animals" mentioned in the book of Revelation of St. John.

The last, sixth group, concerns God, the *Ain Soph*, the Undefinable, the Supreme Source of Creation. It consists naturally only of one element which synthesises all the previous ones containing them all in potentiality.

The "thirty-two ways of wisdom" present in general the penetration of the Creative Power *from above* into the depths of all the different manifestations. It starts therefore from the "Marvellous Reason," or according to another definition from the "Supreme Crown" and, passing successively through all the different stages of penetration, arrives in the last element to the "Reason that rules the movements of the two great luminaries" and to the "Reason that rules the movement of the seven planets" with their respective qualities.

By combining these two systems together, man joined the two halves of the universal cycle. From one side he received revelations from the observation of nature that surrounds him, and from the other side he established a solid base of knowledge under the dogmas taught by religion. Thus the study of these two systems establishes a perfect accord between science and faith. It joins together the two lines on which develops human thought, and the adept who has attained the understanding of these two systems can say that he has effected the synthetic work which reasonable man is predestined to accomplish.

The man who had attained the perfect understanding of all these different Cabalistic systems was called *Baalshem*, which meant "the one who possesses the Name"—the Name of God, which is written in all the innumerable forms of Creation.

PART III

ART AND SCIENCE

CHAPTER I

THE LANGUAGE OF ART

"THERE are still verities buried under the ruins of ancient sanctuaries," said Ménard. It is not sufficient to excavate an ancient monument, to take photographs of it, to describe it from the point of view of its artistic value or its more or less ingenious construction. All this is done and done very thoroughly, but . . . it does not advance us in our understanding of the ancient thought, it docs not unveil the idea of the ancient thinker. Our learned men, though they execute very thoroughly the work of research and give descriptions of ancient monuments, do not pay sufficient attention (or perhaps do not pay any at all) to the symbolism of the monuments of art which we have inherited from antiquity. And yet, if it were otherwise, perhaps we should be able to unravel many enigmas and understand the formation of the primitive writing. This understanding would give us definite proof of the existence at some remote time of *one unique source* of civilisation on earth, it would allow us to penetrate the mysteries of the primitive tongue, or, more exactly, its material expression. In this the monuments of art, judged not only from their artistic value, but from the point of view of the idea that they were intended to express —the monuments of art would perhaps give us the key for which we are searching to open the mythical " Sesame."

I shall try to sketch out before you this new point of view upon art and will show you that no art originated in any one particular country or was confined to it—there is no exclusively French, or Greek, or Egyptian, or Chinese art. There is only *one art* common to the whole earth and expressing a limited number of concrete ideas. What we call by the name of particular art, characteristic of a single country, is only the development in a particular country of one generating idea which can be traced back to a single common origin. I shall prove this by a few examples, from which you will see how an idea developed in a certain country according to the peculiarities of its inhabitants. From the comparisons drawn from different civilisations, which I will put before you, you will be able to see quite clearly the common origin of the primitive idea.

I began this book by a short explanation of Egyptian writing and religion, because, firstly, the so-called Egyptian civilisation is at the base of all the Western cultures and religions, their philosophy, their science, and their art. Secondly, I began with the study of Egyptian writing because it is the only one that we know which has preserved in it, in a perfect form, the so-called ideographic sign, which was the starting-point of writing in general. Other branches of the primitive unique civilisation developed in Eastern languages : the Chinese and the Sanscrit. These two different branches are perhaps as old, or perhaps even older than the Egyptian civilisation, and one is used to consider them as being of totally different origin and having no relation, either with each other or with Egypt. I will show you that this opinion is erroneous and that not only the ideas that formed the basis of art, but even the phonetic expressions rendering a certain thought in these totally different languages, can be traced to a common origin.

From my outline of the hieroglyphic ideographic signs you will remember that the origin of writing was an attempt at the exact reproduction of an object, expressing more or less perfectly its image. The details characterising an object or a being, his particular posture, the accessories that surround him—all this was carefully thought out and presented the exact expression of the idea that the artist wanted to convey by his work. Thus the portrait became the expression of the thought symbolically attached to it, and was quite clear to the one who could read it. You remember, for example, that the name of the god of knowledge, *Sâ*, was written by a partly unrolled cloth, symbolising the gradual process of understanding which unrolls itself before the intelligence of man. This abstract idea which necessitates a long explanation in one of our languages was rendered by one luminous hieroglyph.

The sign of the paddle, *Khrou*, had the abstract meaning of "voice." This might seem at first arbitrary, but if we remember that, according to the teaching the world was created by the word of God, which troubled the surface of the primitive "mass of waters" from which was born the first *movement of life*—the allegory that is attached to the paddle becomes luminous and full of meaning. It is by means of the paddle that the surface of material water is troubled in order to give *movement to the boat*.

Following the development of civilisation, the

primitive symbolic portrait of a thing evolved in art into the ornament which at first sight has no particular meaning. In writing, by a process of simplification, the primitive ideographic sign transformed itself into a limited number of alphabetic letters. These at last lost the symbolic meaning of the primitive glyph, becoming solely conventional signs to mark a limited number of phonetic sounds. The only phonetic writing which, by a very ingenious composition, combined in its letter a certain number of superposed significations—was, as I have shown you, the ancient Hebrew. But certainly it cannot be compared to the hieroglyphs, as it does not possess all the infinite possibilities of the " words of God."

Coming back to art, we must study with the greatest attention the ornament, the architecture, with the particular dispositions of chambers in a building, of columns, the orientation of the building itself, the disposal of frescoes and reliefs, etc. We must not consider that the apparent symmetry of all these elements was the primary cause that directed the architect and the painter. This symmetry must be considered not as the cause, but as the result which manifests necessarily the dominant law of equilibrium, the *Harmony* which, as you remember, is at the centre of the construction of the Universe (the Sephirah *Tiphereth* according to the Cabalists). But all this is theory ; let us come to the examples, and to begin with I invite you to follow me into an Egyptian tomb.

The orientation of passages and chambers, as also the disposal of frescoes and reliefs on the walls—all these details have a deep meaning and cannot be considered only from the point of view of symmetrical ornament. As a general rule, taking for example the tombs of the Ancient Empire at Saqqara, or the tombs of nobles in the cemetery of Thebes, we see an entrance hall round which are painted frescoes representing scenes of ordinary Egyptian life, in which the deceased is either hunting, or fishing, or harvesting, or counting his treasures, etc. In the middle of the west wall and opposite to the entrance, we see a door communicating with a long passage or chamber (as, for example, in the tomb of Rekhmara). On the left wall (the south) we see scenes representing the funerary procession starting from the house of the deceased, crossing the Nile from the east to the west bank (as you remember this journey pictorially symbolised death, which was like the setting of the sun in the West). Then come different complicated funeral rites, the general purpose of which was to facilitate for the deceased the passage through the different fortified gates of the Other World. The procession diminishes as the uninitiated are forbidden to pass these gates. At last only a few high priests are seen accompanying the deceased to the abode of his mortal body. In the west wall of the room is placed the so-called " false door," the one that separates this world from the other. The deceased disappears through it alone, as entrance is forbidden to the living. This is the moment when the god " sun," the prototype of every living being on earth, has actually set behind the west hills. It is the end of life, the burial of the mummy.

Now we turn to the north wall of the chamber and we see the deceased reappearing from the " false door." All the movement on the south wall was oriented *towards the west*—on the north wall it is developing *towards the east*. It is the resurrection, the new life born from death. Thus we see on the

frescoes, scenes of the ritual of " Opening the mouth
and eyes," or in other words of restoring life to the
mummy (which is sometimes replaced by the statue
of the deceased), performed by the priest after the
model of those that were performed by different
divinities for the reviving of Osiris. After long and
elaborate manipulations, pictured on these frescoes,
we see the deceased definitely reanimated, and at last
there appear again scenes of daily Egyptian life that
are practically the same as those portrayed at the
beginning. All this at first glance gives the impression
of perfect symmetry forming a harmonious ornament
round the whole building.

In the tombs of kings of the XVIIIth and XIXth
dynasties at Luxor, we enter by long sloping corridors
representing the passages of Hades which the soul,
having been justified before the court of judges of
the Underworld, has to traverse in following the
" night sun " in order to gain the resurrection of the
morrow. On the walls of these passages are painted
scenes of the so-called book of " What is in the other
world." Chambers of different sizes, communicating
with the principal passage, represent the different
regions of Hades, where diverse tortures were inflicted
on the unjust by gods of more or less terrifying
appearance.

As a general rule the ceiling of a tomb or of a
temple represents the sky. It is interesting to note
here that the hieroglyph depicting the wooden arch
forming the ceiling of an edifice was " PZT " which
depicted by its shape the sign of the sky, " Nut," and
could be interpreted as the " artificial sky."

Thus logically we see on the ceiling the representation of the goddess of the sky, Nut, in her traditional

arched posture. Very often this figure is double to represent the night sky as well as the day sky. Different constellations in the form of animals, serpents, human beings, etc., are grouped respectively under each vault formed by the body of *Nut*. This double picture might seem at first glance to have been painted in this precise fashion only for the sake of symmetry. But this opinion would be erroneous, as the different constellations placed in the two parts of the ceiling show quite clearly the idea of the artist, who wanted to represent the day and night sky.

The same rule of apparent symmetry is carried out in the temple. Take for example the temple of *Apet* where, according to the legend, was born the Theban form of Osiris. We enter through a door in the west wall into the entrance hall. The temple is composed of a certain number of chambers, and the sanctuary " in which lives the god " is in the east end. On the walls we see scenes of offerings and of adoration of the divinity by the Pharaoh or by different ranks of priests. As a general rule all the figures representing the *people*, coming to the temple to perform the rites, or to bring offerings, are oriented from west to east, or in other words, as if they were entering through the door and going towards the sanctuary. On the contrary the images representing the *gods* are painted as if they were *coming out of the sanctuary* and advancing towards the entrance door to meet the devout.

The sanctuary itself is composed of three chambers symbolising respectively the three principal moments of life in the image of the sun : the rising, the zenith, and the setting. The throne of the divinity is naturally placed at the zenith symbolising thus the manifestation of the god in its fullest expansion.

As you see, though the different figures might seem to be disposed in a symmetrical way in order to form an ornament—this symmetry is again only the result of the root philosophic idea which these images must express, and not the cause which would force the artist to dispose them in a particular and harmonious way. In the decoration of an Egyptian temple the figures are the principal element by means of which is expressed the teaching to which the texts are only accessories. It is necessary therefore to concentrate the attention on this principal element of decoration, and it is the study of the figures, of their respective places, of their grouping, as also of the emblems which distinguish them—that unveils the mystery of the creed and of the philosophic conception to which the priests gave this material form.

This method of study often gives much more wonderful revelations than the reading of the texts, and also allows us to penetrate into the secret meaning of the riddles of which very often the religious texts were composed.

In the peristyle hall of an Egyptian temple we see numbers of columns disposed in groups placed at different points of the horizon. The number of these columns has a great importance, expressing the principal rules of cosmogonic mathematics. Indeed, generally speaking, all the various measurements of an Egyptian edifice are of the greatest significance. The motives of the capitals of the columns represent usually the lotus or papyrus flowers in their different stages of development. These flowers were, as we know, considered in Egypt as the emblems of life and we see on some frescoes the " sign of life," the " Crux Ansata," or Ankh, appearing from the petals

Fig. 7.

Nefertoum born out of the lotus flower.

Fig. 8.

(a) Motif of a Greek vase. Racinet, *l'Ornement Polichrome*, p. v.
(b) Statuette of Buddha seated on a lotus. Musée Guimet, Paris.

of a lotus flower. Other frescoes show the birth of the god " Nefertoum " who appears with the morning dew out of the lotus, opening its petals to the rising sun. It is curious to note here that the name of the lotus flower was *NKHB*, meaning literally, a precise material formation born " under the surface " and which " elevates itself," or in other words, the flower which presents a manifestation of the vivifying power, the *Ka* of the plant. We find the same idea concerning the role of the flower as symbol of vital force—in other ancient religions. For example, Buddha is often represented seated on a lotus flower. In the Greek ornament we see the flower in full bloom forming the pedestal for the head of a genius, just as if it had been copied from the Egyptian frescoes representing the birth of Nefertoum.

The capitals of columns of the Egyptian temples, disposed in groups at different points of the horizon, represent the different stages of development of the flower; it is closed in the night, it is in full bloom at midday, and it produces seed at sunset in order to accomplish the cycle of eternal resurrection.

The idea of architecture in Egypt as well as in all other countries had as its origin and objective the exact reproduction of nature. The temple was built in the image of the universe. Thus tracing its gradual development from the primitive idea, through the ideographic sign, to its realisation, we can constitute the following sequence. The observation of the radiant sun shining through the watery sky which is reflected on earth in all kind of vegetative life, was symbolised by the principle of life—*Ra*, the principle of pro-matter—*Nou*, and the result of the action of

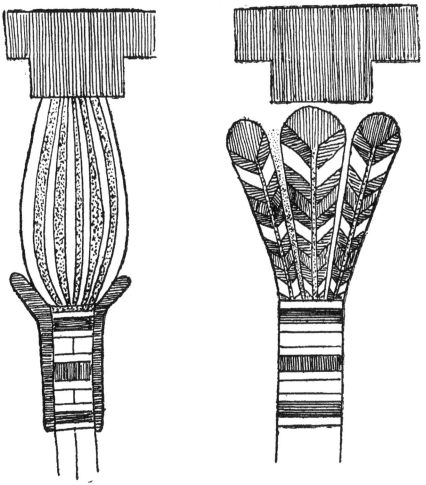

Fig. 9*a*.

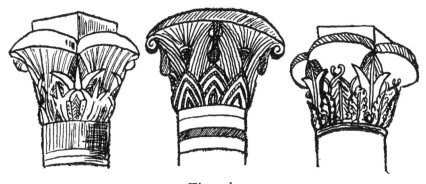

Fig. 9*b*.

Capitals of Egyptian columns in the shape of lotus.

one upon the other—the differentiated life. This life was solidly established between the sky and the earth, and man built the temple to worship God expressing

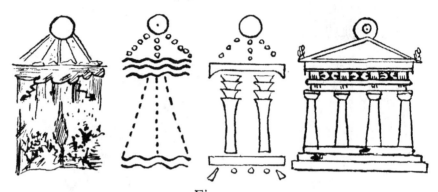

Fig. 10.

The temple—symbol of nature.

exactly the same idea. In Egypt, the temple was covered by a flat roof which symbolised the sky's vault. The sun was represented by the pyramid, or

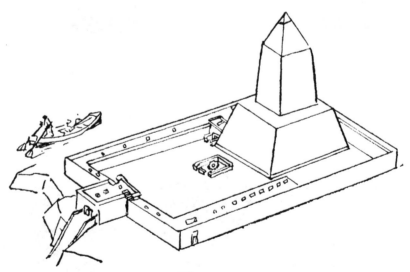

Fig. 11.

Egyptian solar temple.

obelisk, which conveyed the idea of a congealed, or materialised sun ray fixed upon the earth. In the solar temples (such as, for example, the one of Abou

Gourab) the devotee had to walk through long and dark passages and up staircases to arrive suddenly on a platform brilliantly illuminated by the sun. In the middle of this platform was a white obelisk with its point covered with sheets of gold. This sudden change from darkness to the glorious light profoundly impressed the pilgrim, and according to the testimonies of Greek historians, who had visited Egypt

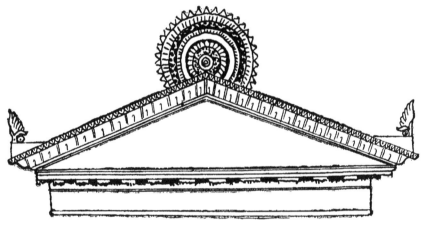

Fig. 12.

The pediment of a Greek temple.

in Pharaonic times—the sight of this shining obelisk reproduced perfectly the idea of a sun ray striking the temple.

The pediment of the Greek temple has conserved exactly the same idea. The centre of it was surmounted by a "rosace" representing the sun disc, or later by a statue of the particular divinity to which the temple was consecrated. The sloping sides of the pediment are reminiscent of rays by which the sun manifests its vivifying action. The frieze supported by columns symbolises the sky, the "waters above." The columns represent the trees, the vegetative life which elevates itself towards the sky, and therefore they were crowned with a flower, the culminating point, the glorious manifestation of vegetative power. The floor and the steps represent the mother earth eternally generated by the father sun to give life to all the innumerable beings on its surface. One understands from this point of view that, when the land was prepared for the building of a temple in Egypt, the priest dug the soil chosen for the future temple and sowed on it seeds. Mentally he associated himself with the work of the Creator and compared the house of God, which was going to be raised from the soil, to the manifestation of life which sprung from the face of earth at the creation.

The tree was, in the belief of all the ancients (example, Druids), the abode of God, as in it was visibly manifested the vegetative power of life.

We see on the Greek temple the ornament called " the Greek wave "; it is placed in the frieze over the columns, in place of the sky of the Egyptian temple; it bears a marked resemblance to the Egyptian sign of water—the undulated line, and it expresses the idea by which Moses defined the sky as the " waters above." We often see the sign of water on Egyptian vases as well as on those of Central America, of Greece and of different Asiatic civilisations. The idea is every-

Fig. 13.

The goddess Hathor appearing from the tree. Tomb of Thiti.

where the same, only its more or less artistic interpretation characterises the sense of beauty and the
capacities of people of different nations. On Egyptian
vases employed in the ceremony of " opening the
mouth " and supposed to possess a vivifying power—
we see the sign of the water over which is placed the
spiral. This gives the word *WN*, meaning, as you
remember, " to exist, to live." In the Greek ornaments

Fig. 14.

The ornament on vases representing water.   Denderah.

we see " the waves " surmounted by spirals which
form the support, or the framing of a flower—symbol
of life. Thus you see that the idea is the same :
life born out of the water and elevating itself above
the surface in the image of the creator Tem, who
" lifted himself above the surface of primordial
waters at the beginning." Again the difference
consists only in the interpretation of this idea by
artists belonging to different civilisations.

In Egypt the lion was one of the solar symbols. In astrology the Zodiacal sign of the lion is the one called " the house of the sun." The god of light was *Shou*, and with his companion *Tefnut*, the two were called the " two lions of heaven." When the first calendar was constituted, the year began with the sign of the Lion in the Ascendant. The previous sign of the Zodiacal cycle which finished the past year is Cancer, which is a water sign, whilst the lion is one of the fire signs. Thus the birth of the new year was naturally symbolised by the *conquest of the element of fire over the water*. We find the same idea expressed in the Hebraic teaching in the formation of the first letter *Aleph* in which, out of the primitive shock given to the surface of water, fire results.

Now in the Egyptian teaching, the goddess Isis (or Hathor), the mother nature, was personified by a cow, the " Celestial Cow," the passive watery element of nature. We can compare this idea with that given in the *Vedas* by the allegorical representation of clouds under the form of cows. In the Greco-Assyrian teaching the mythic rivers were personified by bulls. On a pediment of a Greek tomb (the one of Myra) we see a relief representing a lion fighting with a bull. This artistic picture expresses the same ever-recurring idea of the fight between the forces of life and those of death, or in other words the cycle of life which ends only to begin again. The philosophic development of the idea of constant struggle of the two principal elements : the one of fire with the one of water, or activity with passivity, is found in the cult of Mytra. Another interpretation of the same idea can be seen on some Greek frescoes or vases where in the place of the bull is a horse, the emblem of Poseidon

Fig. 15.

Hathor—the " Celestial Cow." Painting in a Theban tomb.

Fig. 16a.

Fig. 16b.

a. Tomb of Myra. Greece.

b. Ornament on a vase found in Tunis.

—the god of seas, and this horse is attacked by a lion —the fire element.

Another symbol of life, apart from the flower, was the *egg*. We find it in nearly all the ancient civilisations expressing the same philosophic idea. In Egypt the egg, *Sa,* was the symbol of a new formation of life, the son, as the result of a particular combination of natural forces. Osiris in the state of preparing his resurrection had the epithet *SAR*: " The one who is in his egg." On frescoes in Egyptian tombs we see

Fig. 17.

The god Khnum fashioning the symbolic egg.

the deceased in the course of passing through different stages of evolution, framed in an oval forming the protecting shell in the shape of an egg. On other frescoes we see the god Khoum in the act of fashioning the " egg " out of which will hatch the universe.

We can trace the same idea in Greece where the mysterious " Omphalos," representing an egg, expressed the allegory of the birth of the world. In the Brahminic cult we see the god Pradjaparti holding on his knees a cracked egg out of which appears the first couple, the man and the woman. The god breathes into them the breath of life, but it is curious to remark that at the same time he animates by his breath two genii, one of good and one of evil. This allegorical picture expresses the profound idea that the life of man has to develop between two opposing influences and that he will have to make a choice in order to progress or to fall.

Fig. 18.
The egg of Pradjaparti.   India.

This last idea was expressed in medieval times by the Arcanum of " The two ways," where a man was represented standing at a crossing of two roads, a woman dressed in white inviting him to take one way, and a woman in red pulling him in the opposite direction.

Other examples of comparative symbolism belonging to different civilisations might be adduced to prove that at the starting point of all the different interpretations characterising distinct cultures dispersed over the whole surface of the earth—the original idea was always the same.

Fig. 19.

The great Arcanum, " The two ways."

Now I will give you a few examples which show that although writing became in course of time purely phonetic, even in the phonetic itself one can trace the primitive root which expressed, in a particular combination of sounds, a precise idea.

In order that you may not think that in the examples given there might be traced some influence which one language had upon another (a thing that is quite natural if one takes languages of different epochs derived one from another, such as ancient Hebrew, Greek, Latin, which can all be traced either to their Egyptian or Sanscrit origin)—I will take two equally ancient languages belonging to totally different races, which to our knowledge developed each in its own particular way. I will begin by comparing some roots of Ancient Egyptian with Sanscrit, and will proceed to show how the common origin of a glyph can be traced in different writings. For this I will take again for base the Egyptian hieroglyph and will show how the same idea was interpreted in other equally ancient writings.

In the Egyptian hieroglyphic language the letter *R* represents the mouth and expresses the idea of *speech* (Ra—Logos) and also the idea of *sun* (Ra) the centre of light and of heat. In Sanscrit the idea of heat was rendered by the word *Ra*, and the word " to speak " was expressed by the phonetic *Ra-Mh*. It is necessary to note here that the Hebraic radix *Ra* or *Re* has got the meaning of " something dazzling," of a great radiance which is that of the sun. The name of the sun in Sanscrit was *Mytra*, and in Egyptian the word *MTRT* meant " noon," the moment when the sun has developed its power in full, when it reigns in splendour on its throne in the Zenith. Another word used in hieroglyphic language to express the idea of " splendour," of radiance, was *Akhu*, and it was depicted by the sign of the sun emanating its rays. In Sanscrit the word *Aha* meant " daylight." The Egyptian word meaning to join, " to love," was *Mri*, and in Sanscrit the same meaning is rendered by the phonetic *Mara*.

In all the ancient languages it was the combination of *consonants* which formed the root of the word, the vowels entered into it only in order to make it possible to render this combination of " dumb letters " in a sonorous fashion. You will observe that out of all the above examples the original root in these two distinct languages was formed by the same consonants combined in an identical way. Here are some more examples to confirm my postulate. The " *leg* " in the hieroglyphics was pronounced *Pd* and in Sanscrit *Pad*; an " honoured person " was *Bwa* in Egyptian and *Bhawa* in Sanscrit; a " place," a locality, in hieroglyphics was *Bu* and in Sanscrit *Bhu*, and so on. I will not weary you any longer with examples, as I think that those which I have given are sufficient to illustrate my contention as to the common origin of these two tongues, usually considered as being totally different and developed by distinctly separate civilisations.

To conclude this chapter I will give a comparative representation of the solar signs which we find at the starting point of all writings. (Plate IX.)

I append a further table, showing that at the root of the symbolic images of two distinct civilisations was the same principle. The "Twin Lions" of the sky which supported the "Birth Hill" of the solar disc were in the Egyptian teaching *Shou* and *Tefnut*, and in ancient Persia we find a solar symbol composed of two heads of beasts between which emerges the sun. Another interpretation of the same idea can be found in the carvings of ancient Central American civilisation under the form of the "Double-headed dragon," symbolising the two principal events of the day—the rising and the setting sun.

If we take the famous sign of the Caduceus, which is usually considered of Greek origin, we can trace the same idea in the Egyptian solar disc encircled by two serpents in the Phœnician Caduceus, which is the same as in the Hindu symbolism, and which in Chaldea becomes the tree with the serpent encircling its trunk.

These examples have, I trust, made it sufficiently clear that all the art and all the diverse writings of different civilisations on earth proceed from one common origin. Thus, to conclude, we can say that in far-off times of the childhood of humanity there existed on earth *one race* of people who spoke *one language*, and that this language had a creative power presenting, in writing, the exact image of things, and in sound, their constructive vibrations. After

PLATE IX

The Sun in its Different Symbolic Representations

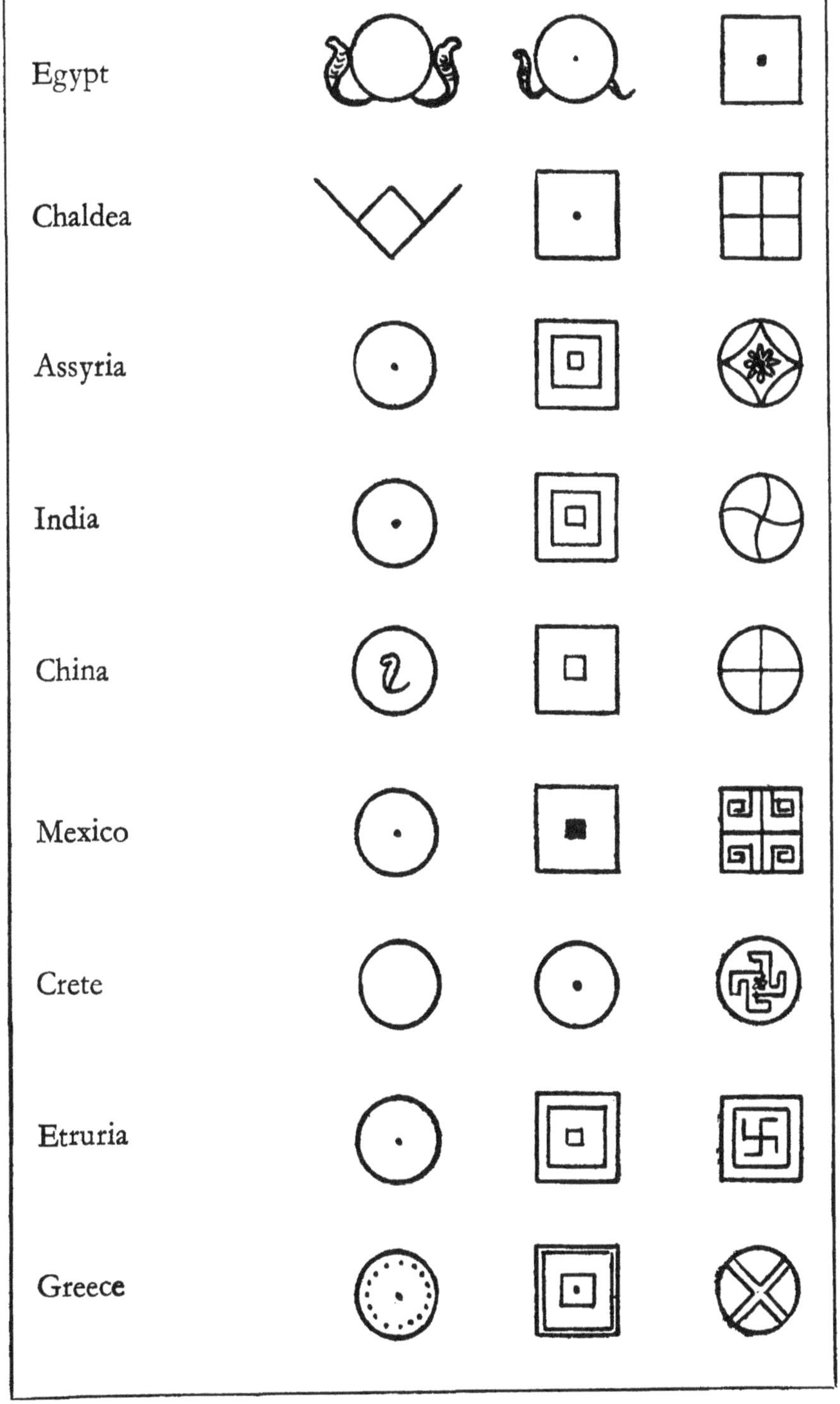

Egypt			
Chaldea			
Assyria			
India			
China			
Mexico			
Crete			
Etruria			
Greece			

Fig. 20*a*.

Fig. 20*b*.

Fig. 20*c*.

Fig. 20*d*.

The two lions. (*a*) *Egypt*—Shou and Tefnut ; (*b*) *Chaldea*—fountain in the rock of Bavian ; (*c*) *Persia*—Solar symbol found at Suze by de Morgan ; (*d*) *Mexico*—Statuette found at Uxmall.

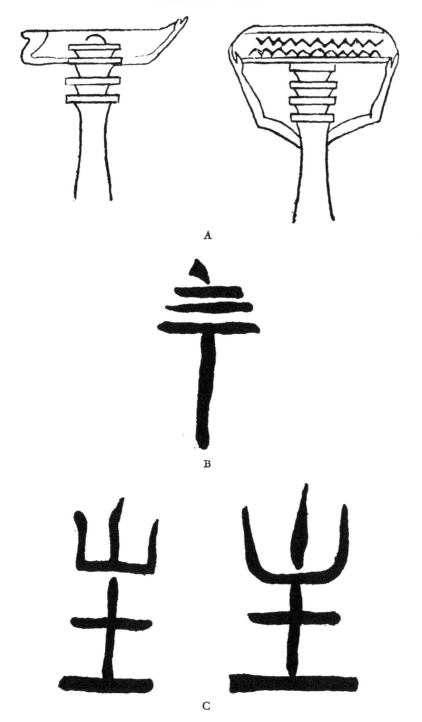

EXAMPLE OF STILISATION OF AN IDEOGRAPHIC SIGN

A. Egyptian hieroglyphic sign *Dad* representing a column and meaning "to support."
B. The sign *Dad* simplified in the hieratic writing.
C. Chinese glyph *Tehou* meaning "to support."

cataclysms like the Deluge, of which we find reminiscences in all the folklore of different races ; after the " mixing of tongues " which followed the destruction of the famous " tower of Babel," the rest of humanity were dispersed over the surface of the earth and started developing their particular forms of writing, and of art, as well as of customs. But the memory of the one primitive idea was strong in all these distinct nations, and it is on the monuments of art that we can trace most easily to its origin this primitive idea which is the same everywhere. This is the reason why it is important to study the diverse monuments not only from the point of view of their artistic value, but also, and this is essential, from that of their symbolic meaning. One must approach each of these monuments with the idea that under its artistic aspect, however striking, is to be sought the primitive teaching it embodies, which it will reveal to anyone who is capable of understanding it.

CHAPTER II

ASTROLOGY

ASTROLOGY is one of the most ancient sciences and we can trace it in all known ancient civilisations : Chaldea, Egypt, China, Central America, etc. In the book of Genesis it is said that the stars were created " to enlighten the intelligence of man." The greatest number of myths which constitute the religion of Ancient Egypt are based upon the allegorical representation of astronomical phenomena. It is natural that human beings were impressed by these phenomena and very early began to remark their rhythmical cycles. The first of these was naturally that of the sun in its daily course in the sky. This observation gave the idea of the intermittence of life and death, the portrayal of which man saw every day in the rising and setting of the sun. The moon suggested to him the possibility of dividing time into periods (months) corresponding to the respective phases of this luminary. The different positions of the sun, according to the seasons of the year, were also observed by man. A statement concerning this observation is found on a statue of an astronomer discovered in Egypt, now preserved in the Cairo Museum. The inscription says that the sage " knew all the changes of the sun—its rising towards the south and its descending towards the

north." This apparently concerned the varying height
of the sun in summer and in winter.

But the observations of the sun and moon were not
the only ones that man had made. His attention was
attracted to the movements of different stars in the
night sky—movements that, as he remarked very early,
were executed round one apparently fixed point on
the sky—the Polar Star. Thus man could establish
in space the four principal points of the horizon :
the east as the one of birth of the sun, the west as
the one of its death, the north as the centre of the
whole sky which he attributed naturally to the
Creator, to the god Tem, and the south which was
opposed to the north point and thus became the
region of the evil god, the enemy—Seth.

All the stars grouped in constellations took, in the
imagination of man, different peculiar forms : those
of animals, birds, snakes, dragons, etc. It is curious
to note that most of the ancient appellations of these
constellations are preserved in contemporary Astronomy, considered as a rational and highly developed
science. But it is important to remember that all the
principles of Astronomy take root in the ancient
Astrology, which therefore must be considered as
the mother of Astronomy. If one examines the names
Astrology and Astronomy one sees that the first
concerns the Logos, expressing that, through observing
the movements of stars, man learned to read the
" words of God." Astronomy means the " reckoning
of stars," and thus defines this science as purely and
solely mathematical. But in all the observations and
calculations of different movements in the sky, from
the most ancient times, one had to use mathematics,
therefore ancient Astrology contained in itself astro-

nomical calculations. We can see the proof of this, for example, in the Cenotaph of Seti I at Abydos, where there existed an elaborate table showing the different moments of ascension of all the constellations known at that time. The exact calculation of the Sothic period of 1461 years and of the Zodiacal year of about twenty-six thousand years, shows the great height to which Astronomy had reached at this remote age. All this is still more astonishing as no astronomical instrument has been found up to the present in excavations in Egypt. There existed apparently a kind of telescope called "MRKHT" and depicted by a representation of a telescope of some kind on a revolving support, but no such instrument has yet been found. On one statue found at Foscat, representing an astronomer, we can observe in his hand an instrument which probably was the MRKHT. Unhappily there is only a small part of this instrument left, the rest being broken off and lost.

Thus it may be concluded that our contemporary Astronomy presents only a part of the ancient science called Astrology, namely, its mathematical part, its frame. In Astronomy all the precise calculations concerned the distances between different stars, their respective movements in space, their dimensions and construction. All this is certainly of value, and shows the great precision of our instruments, but it is not all that can be learned. It is a dry mathematical science, a skeleton deprived of a body and certainly of a soul.

This precision was also necessary in Astrology, but these calculations were not considered as the definite object of this science, but only as an auxiliary, as being necessary to establish it on a solid basis.

The object of Astrology was to study the relations between the different movements of bodies in the sky and life on earth; the influence which the one was observed to exert upon the other thus enabled astrologers to direct the life of man according to the laws " which were written in the sky with letters of flame." Thus you will understand the statement of an Egyptian text in which it is said that " the life on the extreme borders (in the different constellations) is closely joined to the life on earth."

Thousands of years of observations recorded by the sages of antiquity taught them to unravel the mysteries which the different combinations of stars present and to apply this knowledge to the life of man. Thus was constituted the so-called "horoscope" which presents first of all the exact map of the sky at a precise moment, a map traced and calculated according to the rules of celestial mathematics. On the ceiling of the temple of Denderah (as also on those of some other temples) one can see a map of the sky representing the Zodiacal and other constellations in their exact positions at a certain moment which this map defines.

The second part of the horoscope is its reading, that is to say, the application of the deductions of the astronomical problem to the life of man born under particular configurations of the heavenly bodies :

" He traces an horoscope based upon the positions of the stars and he knows the divinities which reign over the destinies . . . he sees clearly into the projects of the Master—what he observes in the sky, he applies on the earth. . . ."

So runs the inscription on the statue of the astronomer already mentioned. This statement seem to define clearly the object of Astrology, which did not stop at observation and calculations, as does contemporary Astronomy, but applied the results of observation of the sky to the life on earth.

Ancient Astrology was composed of two distinct parts : (1) the tracing of a map of the sky at a certain moment ; (2) the reading of this map, that is to say,

Fig. 21.
The Zodiac of Denderah.

the understanding of the influence exerted on man born at a precise moment under the particular combination of stars which happened at that moment. There exists a third element that gives still greater precision to the reading of the horoscope, but we will speak of it later. For the moment we will give a rapid review of the two above-mentioned points, the map and its interpretation.

The horoscopic map presents a circle reproducing in its design the respective positions of constellations of the Zodiac and those of the planets. The circle is divided into "twelve houses," six above, and six below the horizon. The first house is at the "Ascendant," that is to say is *rising* over the horizon at the eastern point. The first six houses are *under the horizon*, the seventh being at the western point opposite the Ascendant. The last six houses are *above the horizon*, the twelfth being just over it in the east, adjoining the first house.

An important point in the map is the *tenth house* which is at the Zenith and which influences all the general orientation of "the theme."

Each house has its particular meaning, thus, for example, the first house contains revelations concerning the length of life of the subject, his temperament, and his character in general; the seventh house is the one which concerns marriage; the eighth death, and so on.

The circle of the twelve houses is immovable, and it is within it that the Zodiacal circle revolves. Thus the first house will be occupied respectively in the course of twenty-four hours of the day by every one of the twelve signs of the Zodiac. The sign that occupies the first house at the moment of birth is said to be in the *Ascendant*, and therefore will influence the whole life of the individual.

Every sign of the Zodiac which corresponds to one of the *simple* letters of the Hebraic alphabet has its particular influence. Thus when a sign occupies a certain house its influence will regulate the meaning attributed to the house. The combination of influences of the twelve signs of the Zodiac in the twelve solar

PLATE X

SOLAR HOUSES AND SIGNS OF THE ZODIAC

Planetary Aspects

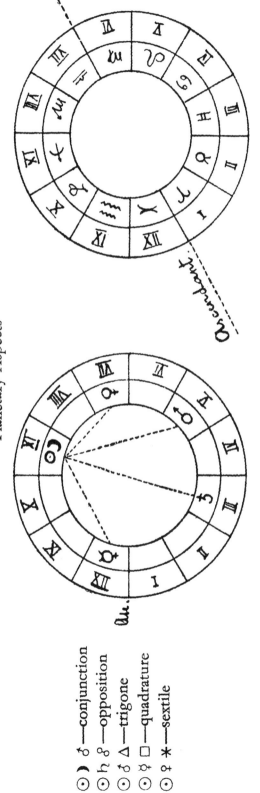

Signs of the Zodiac

☉ ☽ ☌ —conjunction
☉ ♄ ☍ —opposition
☉ ♂ △ —trigone
☉ ☿ □ —quadrature
☉ ♀ ✶ —sextile

P

houses will indicate the general trend of existence for the man concerned in the map, presenting his natural destiny as a consequence of his individual composition.

TABLE OF THE SIGNS OF THE ZODIAC

Aries	Taurus	Gemini	Cancer	Leo	Virgo	Libra	Scorpio	Sagittarius	Capricornus	Aquarius	Pisces
♈	♉	♊	♋	♌	♍	♎	♏	♐	♑	♒	♓

It will also account for the material part of the body of man with the different functions of natural forces at work in it. Thus, for example, a sign of *fire* will give rise to a sanguine nature, and from another point of view will serve as a warning of all kinds of fevers and inflammations which the native must fear. A *watery* sign will exert its influence on the formation of a lymphatic constitution, and the man will be prone to diseases of a dropsical nature. As a general rule the influence of the signs of the Zodiac is inevitable, and we can consider it as forming part of the Karma with which man comes into the world. Remember that the twelve " simple " letters of the Hebraic alphabet which correspond to the signs of the Zodiac were called " simple," because they did not give to man the choice between a quality and a defect which characterises the so-called " double " letters. But one must not draw from what is said the conclusion that Astrology is a science based on fatalism and fatalism only.

In an example taken from ordinary life I will show in what way the life of man is circumscribed by the combination of influences received at his birth. Imagine that you take a berth on an Atlantic liner sailing from England to America. After you have embarked you will be taken to its port of destination, but if suddenly in the middle of the ocean you change your mind and want to go to another port—the liner will not change its course, and you will have to submit to its itinerary. At the same time you are quite free on board to do whatever you like: to eat, to sleep, to dance, etc., but all this *within the limits of the ship*, which will be steadily carrying you to its destination.

The same condition attaches to life; there is laid down a general course for each man to follow which will be maintained throughout, from the moment of his birth to that of his death. In following this course man can manifest his particular individuality, can fight against his defects and can overcome the different obstacles placed on his way, or fail under the tests that put his spirituality to the proof. Thus he will evolve or involve, progress or retrogress.

You might ask: What is the use of knowing beforehand one's destiny if one cannot alter it? The use is great. First of all, man very seldom possesses the knowledge of himself. One of the greatest thinkers of antiquity said: " Learn to know yourself." Usually we see ourselves through a " pink glass," and we are always ready to overlook our defects and to explain them in such a way that they seem insignificant, or even present themselves to us as virtues. In studying the horoscopic map we can not only remark these defects of ours, but also understand their reason, which is clearly revealed to us by the combination of influences that were in action at our birth. From the same study we can trace the misfortunes which our natural defects will cause to us in the course of life. It also indicates most of the infirmities and illnesses of our body. Then, if by studying the map of birth you can foresee what is awaiting you at a certain period of life, you can either avoid an obstacle (in some cases), or at all events prepare yourself for it. As said Ptolemy in his *Centilogium* : " It is possible for one who knows the different influences of the stars to avoid their effects, or to prepare himself for the event."

After one has determined in the horoscope the fatidical, or karmic, influences on man's life formed by the combinations of the Zodiacal signs in the different solar houses—one proceeds to the study of the position of the planets. These last are distributed round the Zodiacal circle occupying separately, or in groups, some of the solar houses. From the first study we have obtained for each house a precise omen or sign depending on the Zodiacal sign which occupies it.

TABLE OF PLANETS

		Sun	Moon	Venus	Mercury	Saturn	Jupiter	Mars	Neptune	Uranus	
		☉	☽	♀	☿	♄	♃	♂	♆	♅	

The planet falling in a house and thus in a Zodiacal sign which is in it, will modify or perhaps change totally the influence exerted by the sign. It might sometimes reinforce the Zodiacal influence. This depends on the nature of the planet being more or less in harmony with that of the sign of Zodiac in which it occurs. The relations between the planets and signs of the Zodiac were carefully studied and defined in ancient Astrology. Each planet had its particular " home," or " throne," in one of the signs of the Zodiac. One sign was called its place of " exaltation," yet another its place of " fall," or " exile," etc. Thus it is natural that a planet occupying its own " throne " or place of " exaltation " would reinforce the influence exerted by the precise sign. On the contrary, if it was in its house of " fall " or " exile "—its influence would be weakened.

Another important feature of the horoscope is contained in the so-called " aspects " between two planets. The aspect shows the respective position of one planet in regard to another, and mathematically will be expressed by an angle. These aspects are called " conjunction " when two planets are occupying the same sign ; " opposition " when they are placed in two opposed signs ; " quaternary " or " square " when they form an angle of 90 degrees ; " sextile " when the angle is of 60 degrees ; " trine " when it is of 120 degrees.

The aspects are regarded as benevolent (for example, the trine and the sextile), or malevolent (for example, the quaternary). The respective places occupied by the planets are calculated astronomically by means of the so-called " ephemeris tables," which give the positions of stars for every hour of the day for a certain year. The aspect that a planet receives from another can either reinforce or change in some way its own particular influence, e.g. a beneficent planet like Jupiter receiving a quaternary aspect from Saturn will change its influence in a maleficent way.

Thus, in short, the influences of a precise solar house will be formed out of the following elements combined together : (1) the particular karmic influence of the sign of the Zodiac ; (2) the one of the planet, or group of planets, occupying the sign ; (3) the aspects received by these planets from others disposed around the ecliptic. These configurations form a complex individual combination for every house in the map of nativity, presenting omens for different moments of life of a subject. Taken together, the twelve houses with their particular combinations express the totality of life of the individual seen from different points of view according to the nature of the different houses.

All these data are obtained by accurate astronomic calculations presenting the exact positions of constellations and planets in the sky at a given moment —the moment of birth of the subject.

This part of the study of a horoscope is called "scientific," or astronomic. But Astrology does not stop at this, as the precision given by these elements is not yet sufficient.

The second part of the study of the map of nativity is purely Cabalistic. Every sign of the Zodiac, as well as every planet, corresponds to one of the letters of the Hebraic alphabet—the first to the "simple" and the second to the "double" letters. Thus the combination of signs and planets in a given house can be considered as a "root," or a combination of roots which have a particular meaning and can be studied, according to the different systems of the Cabala, in their mathematical or symbolical meanings. This study will give a new and more precise revelation and will complete the data of the astronomic calculations. But all these elements give only the particular and complex combination of influences which act at a certain moment and therefore will influence the birth of a certain particular *type of man, but not of an individual being*, as at the same moment and in the same place, there can be born many different human beings. Their lives will be influenced in the same fashion which will differ only according to their respective social position. Thus, for example, the life of the son of a shepherd born at the same moment and in the same town as the son of a king—will naturally develop in a different fashion, though both have received the same general orientation.

In order to obtain revelations concerning the individuality of the subject, one has to study his particular names and titles which place him on a determined step of the social ladder. For this purpose the ancients employed the so-called " Rota " or Wheel of Creation. The Rota presents a circle constituted by the rotation of the name Tetragrammaton, which forms different combinations by the transpositions of letters entering into it. To apply the Rota in order to resolve the problem of a particular name, the letters of the sacred name were replaced by the corresponding letters entering into the names and titles of the subject. This was done by using a special scale in which each letter of the sacred name was considered as governing a group of seven letters of the alphabet. Thus the letters forming a particular name projected like the letters of the Tetragrammaton from the centre along radii into four concentric circles in which they were disposed thus : in the one

nearest to the centre fell the letters forming the first
Christian name of the individual. The omen given
by this circle concerned the spirituality of the man.
In the second circle was written his second or patro-
nymic name. The omen of this circle expressed the
animic part of man, his astral body, or his will-power.
In the third circle was written his family name. This
gave the key to the understanding of the physical
constitution of the man picturing his more or less
perfect body, and on the other hand his innate defects.
In the fourth (external) circle one wrote the titles, or
occupation of the subject defining his social position.

Each of the twelve radii traversed the four concentric circles, and the letters of the different names
of the man disposed along a particular radius constituted a root (or a combination of roots) which was
judged according to the Cabala and tested by the
different systems. The result of this study of all the
twelve radii gave the sum which constituted the
individuality of the man showing all the different
particularities of his character and his aptitudes.

The last proceeding was the application of the Rota
to the horoscopic map of nativity which, as you saw,
gave the combination of Zodiacal and planetary
influences received by man at his birth. Every one
of the twelve radii fell in one of the twelve " houses "
of the horoscope. The root (or roots) obtained from
the respective combination of influences of the stars
in a particular solar house showed the combination
of events which the man had to encounter during his
life. The root (or roots) disposed along the radius
of the Rota falling in the given house expressed the
individuality of the subject. Judged one in regard to
the other, these two opposed combinations showed

clearly : first the different proofs and obstacles that await the man in the course of his life, and secondly how the man will react in all the different circumstances : will he fall under the strokes of destiny ? or will he be victorious ? Thus the last work reveals to the student not only the possibilities of events, but also gives a complete idea of what will actually happen to the man, as in fact his so-called " luck " depends greatly on the particularities of his character. The ancients said that " man is the smith of his own happiness," and this is quite true.[1]

From this short exposition you see that it was reasonable to consider Astrology as a precise science. It was also a " Divine science," as the revelations, which could be obtained by it, lifted the veil hiding destiny. It was therefore naturally in the hands of priests and was taught in the temples to those who were considered worthy to possess the knowledge of reading in the divine book of the future, " sealed with seven seals." Ancient kings used to consult astrologers before deciding upon any serious action. We find testimonies of this in the scriptures as well as in the history of ancient peoples. As we learn from the Gospels, the birth of Jesus was foreseen by the astrologers of the East who came from afar to worship the child who incarnated God.

In our days, so-called " rational science " neglects the teaching of ancient knowledge which it considers as one of the aberrations of antiquity ; yet for the last thirty years one can remark a revived interest in Astrology. A French scientist of the purely rational school, P. Choisnard, after having for a long time studied Astrology and taken careful statistics of

[1] For details see the *Rota*, by the same author.

thousands of observed cases—remarked with astonishment that " the aberration of antiquity " was not so stupid as it was considered even last century. He became the founder of the so-called " scientific Astrology " and an initiator of a big school of students who study this subject in different countries.

But the school of Choisnard takes for basis only the astronomical calculation, rejecting altogether the Cabalistic part of Astrology. Thus the data that the followers of this school obtain are incomplete, not being sufficient to define the individual formation of man, nor to foretell the precise course of events of his life and his reactions to the strokes of destiny.

He who will join to the revelation, obtained by scientific Astrology, the Cabalistic study of the name of the man and of the roots formed by the precise combination of stars—will obtain a complete knowledge of what can be known by man of the future. Thus the deep study of Astrology may not only be useful, but even indispensable to one who is not contented to observe effects only, but who wants to penetrate to the causes which evoke these effects. The study of Astrology certainly requires long and zealous work and a deep knowledge of the Cabala, but the recompense that the student obtains when he possesses this great science is worth the effort that it demands.

CHAPTER III

NUMEROLOGY AND OTHER METHODS OF DIVINATION

YOU remember from one of the previous chapters that the so-called Sephirothic system presented in one of its facets the basis of reckoning—the decimal system. This principle was recorded by Moses in the first ten chapters of the book of Genesis, in which the formation of the universe and its gradual development—the laws of creation, are expounded according to the mysterious powers of the ten numbers. It is obvious that the signification given to the numbers by ancient thinkers will not satisfy many of our learned men, who are used to consider the numbers only in their purely mathematical aspect. They will consider it as a kind of folly to attribute to numbers anything else than the solely physical meaning. From their point of view their opinion seems to be based on facts, and in this they are right, as certainly much has been written in regard to the science of numbers by men who have no idea of the ancient point of view and the real teaching. So I can only associate myself with this opinion concerning these fantastic efforts.

But if there exists a bad musician, can one say that music does not exist, and does not constitute a perfect art ? If in our days the majority of people only know some " fox-trots," or some light melodies and trivial songs, must we conclude that Plato was a liar when he said that music is the key to all sciences? and, remember, this opinion was not only held by Plato, but also by Buddha in India, Kong-Fu-Tze in China, and Woden in Scandinavia—all different thinkers of different ages and separated one from the other by enormous distances—how could they all agree in the same way? Is it not obvious that we have simply lost certain data concerning the comprehension of music? And may we not conjecture that if we could view this art in the way that the Hindus, the Chinese, and the Druids did, we should probably be led to the same conclusions as those they arrived at? It is true that for this understanding we would need other guides than the Italian *solfeggio*.

Plato, who saw in music other things than the musicians of our days see, also saw in numbers a meaning that our mathematicians do not see. He gained the capacity to see this meaning from Pythagoras who had received his knowledge in Egypt. But the Egyptians were not the only people who gave to numbers a mysterious signification. It is sufficient to open any ancient book belonging to any one of the civilisations on earth to see that right from the extreme limits of Asia up to the western boundaries of Europe and America—round the whole surface of the earth—the same point of view obtained. One can give innumerable examples to prove this statement. Must one then consider all antiquity as a lunatic asylum? Can we say that Pythagoras was a madman, Plato a fool, and Kong-Fu-Tze an ignoramus? It would be great impertinence to make such a statement.

Thus if we admit that these thinkers possessed

correct notions, we must admit that there existed at some remote time a language of numbers, of which all the sages of antiquity speak in concert. What was this language and of what did it consist? I will try to answer this briefly.

It consisted in attributing to numbers a certain intellectual meaning, in the same way as one attributes to them now certain definite properties. It is like this. In our days an English mathematician can understand a problem written by a French mathematician in conventional signs; he can resolve it, not necessarily knowing for this purpose the French language. In the same way a Chaldean sage could understand a mystery of transcendent philosophy announced in numbers by an Egyptian, and to do this, there was no necessity for him to know the Egyptian idiom. And as the mathematician knows that the characters that he employs have no quality in themselves, presenting only the signs of forces or of physical quantities—the Chaldean sage knew also that the numbers which he used were only symbols chosen to express forces of nature, that can be understood by man. The profane certainly had a different opinion upon this subject, but a profane man is always and in all things profane.

Not long ago the mob considered the geometrician as a sorcerer; and threatened to burn the astronomer. The mobs of Babylon or of Memphis were as ignorant as those of Rome; not knowing how to distinguish the *sign* that it saw from the *idea* that this sign was supposed to express. Thus the profane imagined, for example, that the number *four* representing the multiplying power of the universe, was this power itself. Many false sages believed this to be so, and misled the ignorant crowd. But for Pythagoras the symbol of the mysterious Tetrad was only a simple four, *when he did not attach to this number the idea of the universal motor.* Just as an x is only an x for the algebraist who does not want to see in it literally the unknown that he is seeking. This is very important to understand. It is just because this important point was not understood that so many unreasonable things were said for, or against, the power of numbers.

This language is absolutely lost in our days, and the error in its understanding is of the same order as the one made in the study of art, which, as I have tried to show in the previous chapter, was also another form of the primitive language.

In the book of Genesis Moses often used this ancient language of numbers. This occurs every time he gives the chronology and seems to fix some dates, or to calculate the ages of persons in his Cosmography. It is curious to observe all the vain efforts of interpreters and commentators of the Bible who wanted to bring these apparent anachronisms into accord. No one of them understood that these numbers were only symbols, and every one forced himself to resolve them according to rules of mathematics. In this symbolic method of expression Moses had given out some of the mysteries of ancient teaching which he could not, or would not, express in another more intelligible fashion.

The so-called " chronology " of Moses represents the world as being only of some seven thousand years old, and one must have a very low opinion of the knowledge of this great sage if one thinks that this was his real belief.

The wonderful proofs of the possession of a

knowledge of the constructive forces of the universe in their gradual development, proofs which we find in the book of Genesis as well as in the books of instruction in the Egyptian temples—all point to the contrary ; that is to say, that the ancient knowledge was much greater than it might seem at first glance. Even the different transcriptions of the Bible (Aramaic, Samaritan, or Hellenic) give different data which show clearly that this part of the work of Moses was much discussed and was a source of controversy even in ancient times. I will not go into the details of comparison of these different texts, and it is difficult for us to understand the reason of these apparent contradictions. Was it the result of efforts to cover these important data with a more occult veil ? Or was it the product of distinct rival schools of antiquity ? —we can only make suppositions regarding these contradictions. Perhaps Hezdra, who banished the Samaritan transcription, considered that it revealed facts that should be concealed from the profane, and the easiest way for this purpose would be to mix up some numbers so as to make them unintelligible. He was perhaps afraid that not only the Chaldeans, but also the Greeks and Phœnicians would be able to understand some of the essential laws which he considered as the inheritance of the " chosen people " only. But these are only suppositions. We have no means of discovering the reason of this apparent disagreement. What we can observe is the evident discrepancies between the three given transcriptions, discrepancies that change altogether the so-called " chronology " of Moses.

It would take too long a time to attempt to explain in detail the symbolic significance of numbers, as it would require the reconstruction of a whole science which is almost entirely lost. Apart from this, such an effort presents a certain danger, as the comprehension of these laws of nature could be exploited for an evil purpose. What we find in the texts is sufficient to put the student in the way of discoveries which will probably astound him.

A careful study of the ten first chapters of Genesis shows at once that each of them bears the character of its respective number. Thus the whole Cosmogony expounded in it forms a complete decade. The rule of the Sephirothic system and also the one given by the Egyptian Ennead is, that the whole development of created forces is expressed completely and definitely in *nine* numbers, the tenth being the synthetic number, the *one* that summarises the maxima of division given by the nine, and at the same time the one that begins the following cycle of nine numbers.

Thus the tenth chapter of Genesis summarises the data of Cosmogony given by Moses, and at the same time begins the part which we can define as Geology.

This needs some explanation, though the previous chapters indicate the way by which the principle *One* developed into *nine* manifestations, which were again summarised by the synthetic unity. This was expounded in my explanation of the Sephirothic system.

The number ten had this particularity in the language of numbers, that it was simultaneously a *final* and an *initial* number. It terminated the first decade and began the next, thus it joined two expressions presenting at the same time the *term* and the *principle*.

1 2 3 4 5 6 7 8 9 10 11 12 13 14 15 16 17 18 19 20 21 22......
 1 2 3 4 5 6 7 8 9 10 11 12 13......
  1 2 3 4......

One sees from this table that the number ten of the first decade is the first of the second, and following the same rule one remarks that $2=11$, $3=12$, and so on. On this rule is based the so-called " theosophic reduction " to the primitive nonad.

As F. d'Olivet states with reason : the first ten chapters of the book of Genesis do not belong to the first decade of teaching, but the chapter which is known to us as the first presents really the tenth of a previous decade. The careful study of this book affords convincing evidence that this is so and that *the ten chapters known to us were preceded by nine other chapters*. A comparison of the statements in the book of Genesis with the teaching of Egyptian temples makes this supposition quite obvious.

The beginning of the book of Genesis, which we do not possess, expounded the Theogony expressing the essence of divinity, as it is found in the sacred books of the Egyptian temples. Having received from the sanctuaries at Thebes these principles of Theogony, Moses judged his people not sufficiently advanced in mental and spiritual development either to understand, or to use, this higher and mysterious knowledge. So he simply suppressed this first part of the primitive teaching, and began his Genesis by the exposition of Cosmogony.

This discovery is of the greatest importance, and the whole book of Moses judged in this new light receives a totally different orientation and value.

So much may be noted as to the theoretical part of numerology. The practical part was set forth in the different systems, such as the *Ziruf* tables, the *Ain-Becar*, the *Magic squares*, and so on. All these systems are based on divers combinations of the sacred name

"Tetragrammaton," which for this purpose was written in a triangle, forming thus the four essential or basic names of God : *I*—the principle ; *Ie*—the first division in two, the positive and negative (the *Mout-f* of the Egyptian teaching) ; *Iev*—the ternary formed of the active and passive principles and their point of equilibrium (the Trinity of Christian religion, or the ternary—father-mother-son of pagan religions) ; and at last the full name of four letters : *Ieve*—the one in which the principle of trinity manifests itself in the quaternary of realisation.   Other combinations drawn out of this graphic formula present the different applications of the sacred name.

The medieval occultists presented the same idea under the form of the mysterious name "Abracadabra," which they wrote in the same fashion in a triangle to obtain the necessary combinations of the image of the name Tetragrammaton.

All these more or less elaborate systems present the so-called *practical Cabala*, and belong to the domain of cryptography.   "This might seem a childish game," as said Eliphas Levy, "but it is as complicated as the most complicated mathematical problem."   This cannot be otherwise, as the science of numbers contains in its symbolical meaning all the essential laws that rule the universe.

Now we will pass to other methods of divination, every one of which in its own way allowed man to lift a corner of the veil which covers the unknown.

The ordinary fortune-teller uses a pack of cards, by disposing which in a certain way he obtains some kind of revelation.   Certainly in this practice there exists a great proportion of fraud, and one can even say that most of these fortune-tellers are only using a certain power of observation and a knowledge of human nature, which they exploit in order to extract some money from the credulous. Yet sometimes in the rubbish that they tell, strange as it might seem, we can trace some part of truth, as if through them you receive a glimpse of the future. One can say this especially about the gypsy fortune-tellers—strange people of unknown and ancient origin, who have preserved in their oral tradition some mysterious knowledge inherited from the old days.

Our pack of playing cards in common use has its origin in the so-called Tarot which presents under the form of a few symbolic pictures corresponding to the letters of the Hebraic alphabet—a whole book, containing in these ideographic images the most secret tradition of antiquity. This tradition could not be entrusted to writing and therefore was expressed in the enigmatic and inoffensive form of childish pictures.

The ancient Tarot was composed of two distinct parts : the so-called *Great Arcana*, twenty-two in number, which corresponded to the twenty-two letters of the sacred alphabet and incorporated the essence of the ancient teaching concerning the Principle and its gradual development.

The second part consisted of fifty-six cards called the *Minor Arcana*, and it is especially from this part that originated our playing cards. The primitive Minor Arcana of the Tarot consisted of four "colours" like our ordinary playing cards, but each colour sequence was composed not of thirteen but of *fourteen* cards. There existed between the Queen and the Knave yet another figure called the "Knight" which in course of time was dropped out of the pack of playing cards. The four colours or suits of the Tarot were: the *Swords*, the *Sceptres*, the *Cups*, and the *Denarii* or *Pantacles*. Each of the colours or suits corresponds to one of the four elements of nature (fire, water, air, and earth) and thus formed the framing of the natural forces, which in Astrology are expressed in the twelve signs of the Zodiac and in the Hebraic alphabet by the twelve " simple " letters. Disposed and interpreted in a right fashion, these cards gave the exact representation of the *karmic* part of destiny which awaited man. In another order of ideas, not being applied to man, the Minor Arcana contained the different *secondary laws* that rule the life of the Universe, but not the primordial Reason and generative forces. These were symbolised by the twenty-two Great Arcana which contained in them the Sephirothic system and all the mysterious revelations which found their application in the twenty-two letters of the sacred alphabet. This is the reason why these last were attached to the Arcana. One can say concerning the Great Arcana that they presented the essence of the teaching, the ideographic pictures in which were symbolised the deepest mysteries of the letters. One who wanted to penetrate to this mysterious meaning had to study the Arcana, and this study gave him the most wonderful revelations. The full exposition of this subject would necessitate long and intricate explanations. I will confine my notes to a summary therefore of the meaning of each of the Great Arcana, considered only from one point of view, but even this short exposition will show the extraordinary possibilities contained in these apparently insignificant pictures. Taken in the natural order of their sequence, according to the one of the letters to which they are related—the reading of their several meanings gives a strikingly logical system presenting the natural cycle of life. In reading the meanings of the Arcana concerning man in the natural order of the letters, we obtain the following aphorisms :

" The free *Will* of man (1) enlightened by *Knowledge* (2) and manifested by *Action* (3) creates the *Realisation* (4) of a power that it uses for good, or abuses it, according to good or bad *Inspiration* (5) in the circle traced by laws of universal order. After having overcome the *Test* (6) which is imposed on man by divine Wisdom, it enters through the *Victory* (7) into possession of the work that the will of man has created, which establishes his *Equilibrium* (8) on the axis of *Prudence* (9) which dominates the oscillations of *Fortune* (10). The *Strength* (11) of man sanctified by the *Sacrifice* (12), which is the voluntary offering of himself upon the altar of self-devotion and of expiation —overcomes death, which becomes the Divine *Transformation* (13) ; thus it elevates man out of the tomb into the region of infinite progress. The immortal *Initiation* (14) is opposed to the eternal *Fatality* (15). The time is measured by the falls, but beyond every *Fall* (16) one sees either the glimpse of *Hope* (17) or the twilight of *Deception* (18). Man aspires constantly to obtain what eludes him, and the sun of *Happiness* (19) will rise for him only beyond the tomb, after the *Renewal* (20) of his being by death that opens before him a large sphere for his free will, for his intelligence and for his action. Every human being who allows himself to be governed by the instincts of the body abdicates his own liberty and imposes on himself *Expiation* (21) of its errors, or of its faults. On the contrary, the human being who joins himself to God, to manifest Truth, and fulfil Justice, enters even during the present life into the participation of the divine Power over other beings and objects—this is the eternal *Recompense* (22) given to the liberated spirit."

These sibyllic aphorisms, presenting some of the symbolic meanings of the Great Arcana (taken in their alphabetic order) outline the course of life for the human being. They show that man is destined to fight his way through the different obstacles and temptations of the incarnated life. The one who overcomes all these obstacles by the constant effort of his will directed by his knowledge, gains the merited recompense consisting of acquired power, guided by wisdom. This same idea was expressed in the Egyptian religion by the combined efforts of the gods *Sa* (the one of knowledge) and *Heka* (the one of magic power) which guide the boat of the sun god through all the ambushes of the underworld.

The twenty-two elements composing the book of the Great Arcana give an innumerable number of combinations. Thus disposed in a precise and particular order to answer a question or to outline the existence of an individual, they will give a precise and deeply philosophic answer. But if to this combination, presenting the individual constitution of all possibilities attached to a particular being—if one adds to this the combination of natural forces expressed by the Minor Arcana—the answer will be still more complete and precise.

It is exactly on this knowledge that was based the ancient method of divination by the means of the Tarot, the feeble echo of which we find now in the common pack of cards.

There exists a great number of other methods of divination, which are all based partly on the observation of facts and partly on the intuition of the one who adopts them.

Thus, for example, Chiromancy, Phrenology, Graphology, are all based on these two principles.

Every member of the body of man bears the particular stamp of his character, which a careful and experienced observer can read. For example, a shoemaker in taking the measurement of your foot could, if trained in observation, tell you with great precision astounding details concerning your character. The foretelling of events by means of these methods is based principally upon logical deduction : man having a certain temperament, certain aptitudes, certain vitality—will probably be faced with certain circumstances in life, which will occur to him in consequence of his particular individuality. The more or less accurate prediction of events depends on the intuition of the fortune-teller.

Another group of methods is employed in the use of the so-called " magic mirrors." To the same group belong the readers in a bowl of water, or in coffee grounds, etc. Those who use one of the above-mentioned methods of divination (if they are not mere frauds) must possess the gift of clairvoyance. In concentrating their eyes on one of these objects they can see the formation of the so-called " astral picture " of an event which has already happened or will happen. It is naturally easier to see an event that has occurred in the past, as everything which has happened has left its impression in the astral. There is nothing magical or supernatural in this ; and every one of my readers is probably acquainted with this phenomenon. What is a photograph if it is not an astral picture fixed on a glass or paper? The event which has actually occurred before the camera has left its impression in every detail on the glass covered with a specially prepared chemical. Man has learned how to develop and fix it on the glass, and that is all. Every object which was a witness of an event bears the image of this event on itself. Only we do not know how to " develop " this image ; for this we have to apply to mediums called " Psychometrists " who possess the natural gift of seeing the impression on things.

Foretelling the future with a magic mirror is more difficult, but it is also possible for anyone possessing the power of " scrying " or seeing the formation of astral pictures. Every event before its actual occurrence on earth is formed in the astral, and the more serious the event is, the more precise is this formation. Thus, for example, one can most easily foretell a death which will strike man shortly, even if at the moment he is in full strength and good health. I had very many convincing proofs of this kind.

To the same group belong, for example, the " blackened nail " or " black spot " in the palm of the hand, used by some gypsies instead of a mirror on which they may concentrate their eyes. In ancient times, for example in Rome, the priests used to study the intestines of the sacrificial beasts, in which they saw revelations concerning the events of the future. History tells us that ancient kings used to consult the guardians of the temples in order to know if they could hope to be victorious, or if they had better abstain from action. In our days in Thibet the lamas examine most carefully bones of mutton which they throw in the fire. I know of cases in which most extraordinary events were foretold in this fashion and came true in every particular detail.

In Egypt some of the " Sorcerers " use for the same purpose pebbles which they throw on the ground into squares which they have traced upon the sand. If you are lucky enough to find a real clairvoyant (and not one of the frauds, which are so numerous), he will astonish you by telling things that seem supernatural and that come true.

But for all these methods of divination, the essential condition is the natural inborn capacity of mediumship. Without this the impression of the astral picture will remain invisible, and it will be only a matter of chance if a thing foretold by one of these fraudulent fortune-tellers comes true.

It is quite otherwise with numerology and the Tarot. In these there is no need of any inborn individual capacities of clairvoyance. The method indicated above is purely scientific; anyone who wants to acquire this knowledge can arrive at its possession. The only condition required for its acquisition is study (long study, it is true), but the result will depend on the zeal that the student will apply to it, and given the effort the result is infallible.

CHAPTER IV

MAGIC

IF one mentions the word " magic " in our days the majority of educated people will smile or turn away with disdain. What is magic in the eyes of the man of the twentieth century ? Only superstition, good enough for people of the olden times in a low state of mental development. Magic is only an aberration, a source of fraudulent living for some crooks who profit by the stupidity and credulity of the simple-minded. This is the general opinion of the learned men of our day, as it is of the one who considers himself as knowing everything.

But if one descends to the primitive sources of antiquity, one is at once struck by the fact that magic played a great role in ancient teaching, and many great thinkers of the earth, belonging to different civilisations, did not consider magic as a lot of superstitions which in our days calumniate the memory of this old science. From the study of all the ancient religions one sees clearly that everywhere magic was at the base of religious teaching, and that it is precisely that so-ridiculed science that was the first human doctrine establishing the foundations of all religious, moral, and political thought.

Certainly many frauds draping themselves in the toga of magicians and pretending that they know the mysteries of antiquity, extract money out of the credulous mob and thus discredit the science itself. But, I repeat, if there is a bad musician, can we say that music is of no account? Or if a house built by a bad architect falls down—can we conclude that architecture in general is a thing of naught? The same argument applies to magic and in a greater degree than to any other science, because magic is mysterious, because it treats of subjects that our rational science considers as non-existent, not having the right to exist, because it cannot be submitted to the few laws that we know and consider as being *the only ones* that rule the universe.

In the present chapter I will try to unfold before you this initial science as it presents itself in the texts which we have inherited from different civilisations. I will also show you by what purely scientific means magical processes can be controlled, and demonstrate that this control shows that there are some laws of nature which were known to the sages of antiquity and which are not even suspected by our learned men.

The name magic was inherited by us from the Greeks who called it Mageya, and the magician Magos. This is an alteration of the terms : *Mog*, *Megh*, *Magh*, which in Pehlvi and in Zend (languages of the ancient East) meant priest, sage, excellent, from which was derived the Chaldean word *Maghdim*, equivalent to "high wisdom," or sacred philosophy. The simple etymology of the word magic shows that in ancient times this science presented all the complexity of knowledge of the ancient " Magi " or philosophers of India, Persia, Chaldea, Egypt, and other countries, who were simultaneously the priests of nature, the fathers of science, and the creators of gigantic civilisations, the ruins of which we admire. In his role of scientist, the magician possessed the knowledge of the laws of the universe, some of which are known to our science.

Thus he was an astronomer, an architect, a doctor, and applied his knowledge in the same way as the learned man of our days does in his particular line of studies. But apart from these physical laws the ancient magician knew also other laws, which we consider now to be supernatural, the existence of which we feel, but which we cannot grip and enframe in the three dimensions, or study by means of any of our instruments. The ancient magician knew how to apply these laws, and how to direct these supernatural forces, which as a matter of fact are not at all supernatural, but inborn in the human being.

The mistake made by our civilisation is that we have largely developed the physical part of our complex being and quite neglected the spiritual part. Instead of looking upwards to the sky, man looks downwards, and all his search is concentrated on the earth. Instead of developing his inborn spiritual qualities, he tries to replace them by a complicated machine, and every ingenious invention fashioned by his hands. Thus, for example, all the new inventions of the last century which accelerate the transport of man from one part of the globe to another, which make him hear or see at a distance—all these were unnecessary to the initiates of Ancient Egypt or India, as distance did not present an obstacle to them. The power of their thought allowed them to see or hear at any distance or to transport their astral body anywhere with the rapidity of thought. The knowledge of the essential laws of nature showed to the sage that there existed a Supreme Reason, the Creator of everything, the One who established all these harmonious laws and who reigns over the universe. Thus naturally the sage became the priest who worshipped the Creator, and for this purpose instituted the creed with its ritual for the initiate. The ritual is a combination of words in the image of the creative Logos, the power of which is at the basis of all religions. The words were pronounced in a precise way, adding thus to the strength of the Logos, evoking the musical vibration which constitutes one of the constructive forces of nature. Then different acts, as, for example, established gestures, the use of ritualistic objects, incenses, etc., were added to the ritual as a means of concentrating the power of the prayer and of creating a harmonious structure in the world of forces. Thus was formed the primitive religious ritual, the principles of which are preserved in all the existing religions, and all these principles were based upon magic.

We find mentions of this science in the religious scriptures of all the diverse races on earth. For example, in the Bible we read about the " Staff of Moses " which turned into a serpent before the eyes of Pharaoh and by the means of which Moses divided the waters of the Red Sea, drew a spring out of a rock, and by elevating which in the desert he cured the plague which was ravaging his people.

If we study the Egyptian texts we see that the high priest used for some mysterious purposes, as, for example, in the ritual of restoring life to a deceased person, a *magic staff in the shape of a serpent* called *Wr-He-Kau*, which means "the great in charms."

We read also in the Bible of the " Staff of Aaron " which blossomed after his prayer; and in Egyptian texts we find the following statement : " The plant blossoms if you call it by its name." I have expounded the belief of the ancient Egyptians who attributed to the name of a being or of an object the meaning of a kind of formula of formation of this particular being or object. Thus *called by its name*, the being or object was created in the world of constructive forces.

But to possess the creative power of the word the initiate was supposed to have the "just voice," *Ma-Khru*, that is to say, that the expression of the name by the means of the logos had to be in harmony

Fig. 22.

The magic staff, Wr-He-Kau. Tomb of Peta-Amen-Ap.

with the forces of nature and not in disaccord with them. The "just voice," *Ma-Khru*, became in the lips of the sage the creative voice, *Per-Khru*, the one which "evoked to life."

We have many testimonies as to the creative or destructive power of the word in the biblical scriptures. Adam *names* the animals, and thus they start their existence in regard to him. "I have killed them by the words of my mouth." (Hosea vi, 5.) And in Egypt the spell against the evil serpent, *Apep*, begins by the words: "That his name should not exist." I only mention these few passages concerning the power of the word as I have already written on this subject in a previous chapter.

The transformation of Lot's wife into a pillar of salt, the destruction of the walls of Jericho by the sound of the trumpets—all these supernatural manifestations mentioned in the Bible are of the order of magic, as also are the different plagues let loose on Egypt by Moses in order to force Pharaoh to liberate his people. We have in the book of Kings the statement that the Witch of Endor evoked the shades of Samuel at Saul's request. One could give a great number of examples showing that magic, as a power or a science, was largely practised in biblical times and considered as a well-known reality. This belief was inherited by the Hebrews from the Egyptians. In Egypt there existed a god of magic power, called *Heka*. In all the texts, right from the first known, those of the Pyramids, we see that magic constituted a great part of religion, and that the deceased was provided with a " knowledge of the names " of the gods of the underworld in order to be able to pass through the different gates which they guarded.

Magic was largely practised in the Egyptian temples, and in the religious texts we read a great number of formulæ to conjure either venomous living creatures like serpents, or scorpions, or evil spirits, or elementals. For example, in the tomb of Ankh-Ma-Hor at Saqqara one sees on a wall a representation of the crossing of a stream (or a channel) by a herd of oxen driven by two men in boats (the herd crosses the water by a ford). In order to protect the animals from the attack of crocodiles, the herdsman standing in the bows of the boat pronounces a magic formula and extends his hand over the water. This double action, as is stated in the text written near the picture, " enchains " the crocodile, paralysing his movements ;

and we see the picture of a huge crocodile lying under the surface of the water in a posture showing that he is arrested in his movement.

Herodotus testifies that the army of Senaccherib was stopped in its advance towards Thebes by an epidemic of plague which destroyed the whole army, and from the explanations given to him by the hierophants he ascertained that this epidemic was brought about by means of magic. It is curious to note here the method employed in this particular case by the Egyptian sages. They exposed on the walls of the city a " golden rat," which being consecrated in a particular fashion provoked this terrible disease in the enemy's camp.

I consider this as affording striking evidence of the deep knowledge that the Egyptian priests had of the propagators of the microbe of plague. It took our learned men some thousands of years and a perfect development of bacteriology to find out that it is through *rats* that the plague spreads. Why did the Egyptians use the image of a *rat* and not of some other kind of animal in order to evoke this special epidemic? I leave it to you to solve this *coincidence*, if it can be considered as a coincidence.

I have already mentioned the magic pictures and statuettes coming to life by the force of the word *Per-Khru*. There existed a certain form of funerary statuette called *Oushabti* or *Shwabti*, a word that is derived from the verb meaning " to represent," to replace. The belief was that the deceased had to execute different kinds of work in the underworld, and in order that he might avoid this trouble he was supplied in his grave with Oushabti statuettes. These were prepared in a certain ritualistic way and were consecrated by a special magic formula. The idea was that they would *come to life* at the call of the deceased and accomplish the work to be done in his stead. In tombs of rich people one finds great quantities of these Oushabti figures, but even the poorest peasant had one or two Oushabti, fashioned in clay, or carved in wood, which were buried with him. Under the name of Oushabti or Shabti, the Egyptian understood everything that was prepared in a certain fashion and that executed work instead of man. Thus, for example, the water-clock (*clepsydre*, according to the Greeks), which was employed to measure the hours of the night, was called by the Egyptians a Shabti.

For the treatment of some diseases they employed a special necklace of beads, which served to take away the disease and " drop it on the ground " (papyrus Ebers). This necklace was called also a Shabti, as *it executed the work for the medical man*.

One must distinguish from the Oushabti statuette the so-called " *Ka* statues." These were carved to represent more or less accurately a portrait of the deceased. By a special magical process the priests attached to this statue a part of the soul of the deceased, called the *Ka*, or according to the definition of Maspero, " the double of the man." One of the most interesting of these statues is the one of the King Hor, now in the Cairo Museum.

The magic formula in the hieroglyphic ideographic language was represented by means of a knotted rope. The way by which the symbolic mother, the vulture *Mout*, sealed or attached the name to a particular man was expressed by the sign *Shn*, which represents a rope the ends of which are strongly bound together. The so-called " cartouche," or oval, which surrounds the signs forming the name of the Pharaoh, is a variation of the same sign. The " Crux Ansata," or *Ankh*, called " the sign of life," is also a magic knot tied in a particular fashion.

This is quite logical, because according to the belief of the ancient Egyptian, the complex being of man was formed of *nine* distinct parts, which were all bound together, and this binding constituted his individual life. Another meaning of the same sign which is in close connection with the previous one is to be traced in the word " horoscope." We find this sign employed in this meaning, for example, in a text written on a statue of an astronomer, where it is said that " the life (*Ankh*) of men is tied up with the life (*Ankh*) of the stars." Here, the sign *Ankh* expresses again the meaning of knot, " the knot of destiny," which was tied in a certain individual fashion in order to give man a particular form of existence on earth.

The priest possessed the knowledge how *to tie* by means of magical proceedings a part of the personality of man to an object, and in the case that interests us this object was the so-called *Ka* statue.

This ought not to astonish you. Probably all of you have read about numerous medieval processes of so-called "Bewitchments," when sorcerers employed, for the purpose of destroying someone, specially prepared and consecrated wax statuettes representing the features of the person they wanted to harm. Many sorcerers were burned for the exercise of these evil arts. The learned men of our rationalistic epoch laugh at such things, and say that they afford further instances of the aberrations of a time when people lived surrounded by all sorts of superstitions.

Yet in the beginning of this century a French

scientist, Colonel de Rochas, who for many years experimented upon subjects plunged into the deeper phases of hypnotic trance, demonstrated before scientists in Paris the exact reproduction of this medieval experiment in every slightest detail, with a wax figure. For this purpose he hypnotised his subject, putting him in a deep stage of hypnotic sleep, when his vital force could be exteriorised. Then he attached a part of the vitality of the subject to the wax figurine, and when the patient was awakened, he retained an imperceptible link with this figurine. This last was, for example, taken away to another town, and when it was pricked with a needle in certain spots, the subject felt pains and exhibited red marks on the corresponding parts of his body. It would take too long to recount in detail all the extraordinary experiments made by de Rochas, at some of which I had the good fortune to assist. Those who are interested in these questions will find detailed accounts of the experiments in the works of this scientist.

Another maleficent proceeding of the same kind was formerly performed in India, and I believe that it is still practised. It is called the " Stabbing of the shadow." The sorcerer watches his victim, and when he sees its shadow on the ground at a certain angle he stabs it in the heart, pronouncing a special formula at the same time. The effect of this, when performed by a real sorcerer, is death at the appointed moment chosen by the magician, but the body of the victim bears no trace of the murder.

In some tribes of Central Africa the witch-doctors use for the same purpose of harming an enemy some of his excrements which they heat with a special ritual and formula. This provokes an internal disease, fatal to the one who does not know how to undo the magical knot of the bewitchment.

I will content myself with these examples of the low, or as they call it, " black magic," which is much more prevalent than people think, and which constitutes a great danger. It is a fortunate thing that in order to do anyone harm the sorcerer needs to be in possession of something representing part of his victim's body, as, for example, his blood. This is not often easy to obtain, otherwise we should all be at the mercy of the evil and unscrupulous scum of humanity. It is also a very dangerous thing to allow anyone to hypnotise you, as the hypnotiser obtains a certain power over his subject, which he might be tempted to use for evil purposes.

One of the most mysterious rituals of ancient Egypt was the so-called " revival through the skin." Mention of this ritual is found in the texts of the Pyramids as well as in the solar temple of Abu-Gourab described by von Bissing. In certain tombs of the New Empire in the necropolis of Thebes we find pictures representing different stages of this ritual. Briefly, it consisted of the following processes. It was believed that youth could be regained by the means of enveloping the body of an old man in a skin stripped off a human being, or later of an animal. The so-called " festivals of Heb-Sed," which were regularly performed for a Pharaoh during his reign, were based on the same principle. This belief had for basis the myth of the fight which took place between the gods Osiris and Seth and in which Osiris was killed and cut to pieces by his enemy. The body of Osiris was restored by the two goddesses,

Isis and Nephthys, symbolising, as you remember, the two opposite forces of nature—the one of evolution and the one of involution. In order to join the parts of the restored body together, Anubis, the son of Seth, the jackal, gave his own skin (called *Out*), in which he enveloped the body of Osiris. This skin was the prototype of the mummy swathings, and the god Anubis was considered as the one who taught men the way of preserving the dead body.

Thus, in accordance with the process described in this legend, in olden times they used to kill an enemy symbolising Seth, during the festival Heb-Sed, and his skin served to give new life to the Pharaoh. Later when religion became more moral, the human sacrifice was replaced by the killing of an animal, of the kind which was considered as belonging to Seth (the panther, the hyena, the gazelle). Thus we can account for the appearance of the so-called " spotted skin," which was used by the priests in the course of the ritual of reviving the deceased. On many frescoes we see the priest called *Ywn-Mout-F*, or " the one who possesses the mystery of life by combining the two principles : the one of the father and the one of the mother," wearing the " spotted skin " over his shoulder, showing the means by which this mystery was performed.

Another proceeding of the same kind was based on the solar myth, in which it is said that " the sun is born every day from its celestial mother, the cow, Hathor." Thus, in order to reproduce this myth the patient was enveloped in the skin of a cow (the *Mesqa* or *Meskhent*), which acted symbolically as the womb of the mother for the child. The skin of a cow, or of a bull, was considered in different civilisations as possessing a generating power. We see in the Egyptian texts (for example, in the tomb of Seti I) that out of it " are born bees and grasshoppers," these beings represent the first manifestation of individual life. In the Greek teaching we find the statement that " the bees are born from bulls." (Porphyre, 1, *Antre*

Fig. 23.

Painting on a ceiling of an Egyptian
tomb. Cairo Museum.

des Nymphes.")   According to the ancient teaching the bull was the symbol of generating power (the *Ka*, according to the Egyptian texts). In Egypt we find on certain ceilings in tombs (one can be seen in the Cairo Museum) an ornament representing heads of bulls surrounded by spirals in which are formed larvae of primitive beings. It is curious to note the belief which reigned in prehistoric Russia, and according to which "the spirit of the woods threw a horse into a swamp and out of its skin was born the beehive."

We find in the Brahmanic religion a ritual called the "Digša," which has many similarities with the Egyptian *Heb-Sed*. The Digša was considered also a powerful means of restoring vital force to a man fallen into decrepitude. For this purpose a pavilion was erected (like the pavilion of *Heb-Sed* in Egypt) and in it the patient was enveloped *in the skin* of a black antelope. (I refer those who are interested in

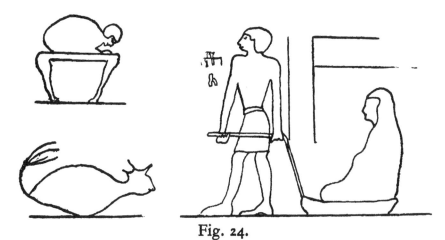

Fig. 24.
The Tikenu.   Tomb of Mentu.

the details of this procedure to the marvellous book of Sir James Frazer, *The Golden Bough*.)

In the Egyptian religion the ritual of revival by means of the skin evolved gradually from the barbarous custom of human sacrifice, which was in vogue in prehistoric times, to a purely symbolic ritual, in which the actual sacrifice was replaced by magic formulæ. The stages of this evolution can be traced as follows. Firstly it was the patient himself who was enveloped in the skin; later he was replaced by a youth called the *Tikenu* who acted in the place of the patient and in olden times was probably killed at the end of the ritual. Later still the youth was replaced by a dummy, and at last it was the officiating priest *Sem* who acted the part of the *Tikenu*, enveloping himself in the skin (or a cloth representing the skin) during the funerary ceremony. We see the representation of this part of the ritual in many tombs of the New Empire, for example, in that of Seti I, of Rekhmara, etc.

To conclude, we can say in general that the Egyptian religion consisted in olden times principally

Fig. 25.
The weighing of the heart. Pap. Ani.

of magic ritual. It was believed that only by knowing the names of the divinities of the underworld could the deceased force for himself a way to the Elysian fields. Later, with the spreading of the Osirian teaching, morality predominated over magic, and man had to prove a "just life" in order to attain to paradise. Allegorically, this was represented by the scales on which the heart of a man was weighed after his death. One sees on frescoes of tombs and on numerous funerary papyri a representation of this scene. On one tray of the scales is placed the heart, and on the other the feather of *Maat*, the goddess of justice. This pretty metaphor expressed the idea that the heart of the man had to be " as light as a feather," or in other words : sinless. A court of judges was seated in the same scene and carried out the sentence. The god Thoth acted as the advocate of the dead. After the sentence was decided upon by the jury, the dead was brought before the supreme judge of the underworld, the god Osiris, who sacrificed his own life in order to serve as a prototype for the human race. Osiris appointed to the deceased his place in Hades according to his state of perfection or imperfection. Thus the just was glorified and the unjust punished.

The different texts of moral teaching, as for example the " Admonitions of Amenemhat," " The Precepts of Ptah-Hotep," and those of Prince Merikara—all show a very high standard of morality attained by the Egyptians in the course of time which approached very closely to that of the Christian teaching.

But though magic seems to lose its predominant place in religion, it nevertheless was conserved in the teaching and we can see that, next to moral principles, the different magic proceedings, preserved from ancient times, were believed to help man in his progress. Thus magic was never considered as being opposed to religion, and was not banished from ancient temples. It is only in medieval times that magic was considered as the science of the devil, and this opinion was well based, for the kind of magic that was practised in these times was not the high and purely religious magic of antiquity, but the low and dangerous sorcery which employed knowledge of some natural forces only for vile and entirely materialistic purposes.

One must not confound magic either with spiritism,

so much practised in our days, nor with conjuring or the feats sometimes performed in circuses and music-halls. The results obtained through the practices employed in both these proceedings (if they are serious and not simply a fraudulent way of extracting money from credulous people) present an action of natural powers inborn in man and having nothing to do with the other world. They are based either on mass hypnotism, or on transmission of thought which seems supernatural once it is formed on the magnetic field exteriorised by the medium. Thus, for example, all sorts of levitations, of noises, and of luminous effects observed during spiritualistic séances —are only due to the magnetic, or vital power exteriorised by the assistance, and condensed by, the medium. All this is very interesting as a proof of forces that are inborn in man and not yet defined by science, but one must not infer that they present proof of communication with spirits.

The same can be said about the sometimes wonderful performances of fakirs, which are in general different forms of manifestation of the power of suggestion, or mass hypnotism. Thus, to take a well-known experiment, when a whole crowd sees a monkey climb up a rope thrown up in the air. When photographed, the negative showed the monkey sitting on the shoulder of his master, who held the coiled rope in his hand. Magic is in quite a different category. It is purely scientific, and requires very long study in order to obtain the necessary knowledge of natural forces. It demands also a special preparation from the adept, which makes him worthy to penetrate into the secrets of nature. He must develop a strong will, sharpened like the steel of a sword, for it is only by

PLATE XI

𐎧 shn - to tie

𐎧 shs - to untie

𐎧 𐎧 Shn - magic conjuration

𐎧 - Shn - the seal, the knot

𐎧 - Rn - the Cartouche surrounding the name.

, 𐎧 𐎧 𐎧 - Heka - magic formula.

𐎧 𐎧 𐎧 𐎧 𐎧 Wr-he-kau - magic staff - " the great in supernatural power".

𐎧 𐎧 𐎧 𐎧 𐎧 𐎧 - Hekau - magician sorcerer

𐎧 𐎧 𐎧 Sed - the tail, ritualistic sign attached to the belt of the pharaoh and high priest who had received the initiation.

𐎧 𐎧 𐎧 honorary title of the function of the priest Sed

𐎧 𐎧 𐎧 Heb-Sed - pavilion erected during the jubilee of initiation of the king

4. 𐎧 𐎧 - Wt - the skin of Anubis - prototype of mummy swattings.

𐎧 𐎧 𐎧 Ymiy-Wt - the one who is in the skin Wt (who is about to be revived).

𐎧 𐎧 Wt ynpou - the priest of the funerary ritual, the embalmer.

5. 𐎧 - Ms - the three skins bound together

𐎧 𐎧 𐎧 - to give birth, to be born

𐎧 𐎧 𐎧 - child.

𐎧 𐎧 - Mesku - the skin of birth.

𐎧 𐎧 𐎧 - Mskhent - the stool of birth the means to give birth.

𐎧 𐎧 𐎧 𐎧 Mskhet - the thigh, the constellation of the Great Bear - the means of realisation of the universe.

6. 𐎧 𐎧 𐎧 𐎧 - Oushabti - the delegate or the answerer, written otherwise 𐎧 𐎧 𐎧 𐎧 the royal offering, the one that represents the king before the god.

means of this that he can put into action the results of his study. Thus magic is simultaneously a high religion, the deepest science, and gives the one who is in possession of its secrets a power which can be considered as supernatural. A true magical operation can be tested by all scientific means in our possession : by photography or by any other form of record made by a machine, which cannot be suspected of being affected by suggestion. Very interesting experiments carried out by Sir William Crookes in the last century proved with certitude the reality of some phenomena of mediumship. I myself have many times tested different supernatural manifestations and could thus separate what is reality from what seems to be so to the observer.

Thus I can assure anyone who wishes to experiment in this way, that *magic is a reality*, but that one must never accept the apparent phenomena as real and not being caused by an aberration of the senses. Such an one must put every manifestation of this kind to a very severe and scrupulous test. Only on this condition can one obtain certitude. It must not be forgotten that *magic is not a creed but a science*. In the former belief is sufficient, in the latter one must start with doubt and try to explain by means of physical laws what might seem to be a supernatural manifestation. Accept a phenomenon as being magic only after applying tests and obtaining proofs that eliminate all possible doubt.

CHAPTER V

MEDICAL ART

IT is generally considered that China is the cradle of medicine as a science. One of the most ancient documents that was known up to the beginning of this century is the medical treatise written about 2700 B.C., during the reign of the Emperor Chin-Nong. It was believed that the notions in medicine of the Chinese, spreading through Asia, were imported into Egypt and then to Greece. Greek philosophers, Pythagoras, Empedoclos, and Democritos, who all received their initiation in Egypt, founded a school of medicine at Cuidos. The students of this school were taught how to diagnose the different illnesses. Another school, founded at Cos, and directed by Hippocratos, studied different methods of treatment of diseases. These treatments were based mostly on the prescription of a rational diet and on different natural methods, as, for example, gymnastics. As medicines, different herb-teas, honey, etc., were employed.

Later, with the foundation of the medical school in Alexandria, scientists such as Herophilos and Herasistratos started the study of anatomy of the human body, which was later developed by Galienos. This last, by dissecting corpses, could not only delineate the exact formation of the human skeleton, but also describe the different functions of muscles, of arteries, of nerves, and of certain glands.

Thus our contemporary medicine ascends to the so-called " Asclepiades " or priests of the cult of Asclepios, called by the Romans " Esculapius"—the god of medicine. This name is a corruption of the Egyptian name Im-Hotep, who was the god of medicine in Egypt, worshipped during the New Empire. In Egypt are temples consecrated to this god at Philæ, the one built by Ptolemeos Philadelphos,

Fig. 26.

Im-Hotep, Egyptian god of medicine. Cairo Museum.

the one of Deir-el-Medinet, and another near the Temple of Rameses III at Medinet Habou.

We have every reason to suppose that Im-Hotep, considered as a god in the time of the New Empire, had really lived. Some inscriptions of the Old Kingdom state that Im-Hotep lived at the time of King Zozer (IIIrd dynasty, over 3500 B.C.), and was simultaneously the court chief doctor and architect. We have reason to suppose that he was the builder of the so-called Step Pyramid at Saqqara, in which was buried the King Zozer. These combined functions may have nothing in common one with the other, but all science in those days was concentrated in the temples and the priests were simultaneously worshippers of god as well as scholars.

Allusions in some medical papyri found in Egypt make it certain that already in the time of Im-Hotep there existed medical treatises, written perhaps by this great master himself, or perhaps even anterior to him.

The documents concerning medicine, found in Egypt, as, for example, the papyri Ebers, Hearst, the one of Berlin, and the one of London, consist of different prescriptions in which oil, honey, and other ingredients constitute the essential part of the medicament. In them are different purely magic formulæ by which a disease was conjured. A papyrus found by Edwin Smith in the beginning of the present century and published recently by Professor Breasted stands quite apart from all the mentioned papyri. It presents a scientific surgical treatise composed in a way similar to the one adopted in our days for works of the same kind. It consists of a certain number of cases described systematically ; each presenting first the description of the case, then the diagnosis of the medical man, and lastly the prescription of treatment which has to be carried out. Unhappily a great part of this most interesting document is lost, but from the fragment which we possess we see the rational and purely scientific composition of this treatise. It begins with different injuries of the head, then goes down to the neck, shoulders, breast, and probably was continued in regard to the whole body. It is natural to suppose that this treatise presented a course of medicine taught in the ancient Egyptian medical schools. That such schools existed we have got a definite statement, though of a rather late epoch (about 500 B.C.), from which we can judge that the school in question was only restored at the time mentioned, restored to the same state in which it had been before. "I have made according to the order of His Majesty," says this document, "I equipped two houses with students

chosen among young men of good families. . . .
I equipped them with all the instruments mentioned
in ancient documents and with all that was there in
old days. . . . His Majesty made all this because he
knew the value of medical art directed to save the life
of any one seized with an illness." (Statue of Ousa-
Hor-Rasemet, now in the Vatican Museum, Rome.)

Thus we can say with certainty that our contemporary medicine was developed from the Egyptian
medical art which was imported to Europe by the
Greeks. The antiquity of documents referring to the
time of Im-Hotep proves also that the opinion that
medicine originated in China and was imported to
Egypt, is without foundation, as some of the Egyptian
documents are anterior to those of China by at least
a thousand years. But we can say again that it is
very probable that the previous knowledge reverts
to a common root of the one primitive civilisation
on earth, and that later this knowledge developed
separately and along particular lines in the two ancient
civilisations—those of China and of Egypt.

The foregoing summary was necessary in order to
establish the fact of the antiquity of medicine, and of
the origin of the principles forming the basis of our
contemporary medical science. Now I will come to
the essential point that distinguishes the ancient
conception from the one accepted by our rational
learned men.

I have said that in ancient Egypt, next to the
rational methods of treatment, which do not differ
very much from those adopted in our days, there
existed a distinct and very developed branch, which
can be defined as " magic treatment." For example,
we find in Egypt the so-called " healing statues "

which were in vogue in ancient times, and many of which can be seen in museums. The majority of these represent a stela of different sizes, varying from a large one (a foot or more high) to a small pocket stela, or even an amulet. They represent the so-called

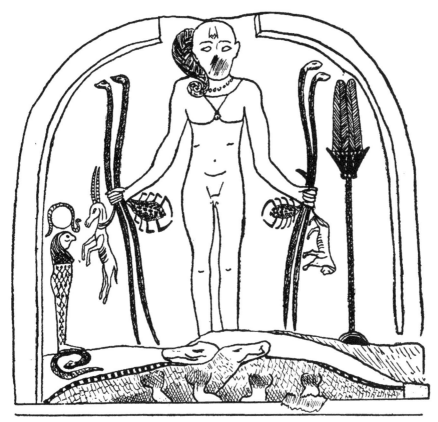

Fig. 27.

Horus the Saviour. Cairo Museum.

"Horus the saviour," and are covered with inscriptions constituting prayers and magic formulæ. A stela of this kind was dipped in a basin of water and then this "consecrated water" was either drunk or applied externally for different ailments or injuries. It was believed that by contacting the magic inscriptions the water received a curative power. One can see in the Cairo Museum a statue of a doctor, Zed-Hor,

s

entirely covered with magic inscriptions and having a basin at its base. On these inscriptions one reads that this medical man, renowned in his time, had his statue made during his life in order to serve by his knowledge all those who suffer from different diseases. To be cured, they had to pour water on this statue and collect it in the basin at its pedestal. The last was engraved with inscriptions ; and their actual state shows that it was largely used, as the inscriptions on the basin are much worn.

The learned man of our days smiles and judges all these magic proceedings as due to the aberrations of antiquity. He is only interested in the rational methods of cure adopted in the old days, and rejects with disdain what he considers as childish superstition. And yet before doing so one ought to penetrate more deeply into the conception of the sages of antiquity and try to ascertain their point of view.

In the previous chapter I have tried to expound the real meaning of magic as a science based on the knowledge of the constructive powers of nature. In order to be able to understand the different magical processes employed by the doctors of ancient Egypt we must try to conceive their point of view concerning the constitution of the human being. If we do so perhaps the seeming aberrations and superstitions will present themselves as not so foolish as they seem at the first glance.

The medicine of our days departs from the postulate that an illness affects only the human body, and it orients all kinds of treatment to paralyse the destructive action of different microbes which have been found by bacteriology.

Thus it might seem that the medical man of our

days considers, *a priori*, that man presents only a physical body and that the causes of all the affections can reside only in this material vehicle. The ancient teaching believed that man was a complex being composed of the material part (the body), of a combination of natural forces (the soul), and of a spiritual part (the spirit, or the divine spark), which is the real seat and source of life. The Hebraic Cabala called these three parts respectively: *Nephesh, Rouah*, and *Neshamah*.

The being of a man in good health presented in the eyes of the ancient sage a state of perfect equilibrium of the three parts composing his individuality. An affection of some sort was a proof of a disturbance of this equilibrium, and it was for the sage to find out the reason of this last; and to try and restore the lost equilibrium. This was the starting-point of diagnosis for the ancient doctor, and in this the ancient medicine differed from that of our days. It is natural, therefore, that the methods employed by the ancient sage were different. They can be divided into three distinct groups. The first concerned all affections of the body, as, for example, all kinds of injuries, some internal diseases, etc. The second concerned the disturbance of natural forces in man, or in other words, all kinds of obstructions and nervous affections, or as occultists would call it, disturbances of the " aura " of man. The third group presented different spiritual affections of the order called now mental illnesses, embracing all kinds of madness, or insanity.

The means employed to reconstitute the equilibrium in any one of these three distinct parts naturally differed in each case, and some of them seem to us as belonging to the domain of pure magic. It is comprehensible that in order to cure an affection of the body the ancient doctor, like the practitioner of our days, employed different kinds of medicines which were prepared either from plants or from mineral chemicals. Thus, for example, in Egypt a great part of the latter consisted of different combinations of soda known under the name of " Natrum." We learn, for example, from the papyrus Edwin Smith, that the best way to accelerate the healing of a wound was to apply to it fresh meat which was bound to the wound " only for twenty-four hours " as states this document. This proceeding is well known in the so-called " country medicine " all over Europe, and I may state that I have known of many cases in which it was employed and gave most satisfactory results.

Astrology also played a great part in the establishment of the correct diagnosis. The study of a horoscopic chart of a nativity, and more particularly of the so-called " revolution," or map of planetary influences at a precise moment in the life of man—showed clearly the different planetary combinations in action either at the birth or at the moment of the affection. Thus the astrologer could see the fatal combination of influences, which had caused the disequilibrium and so could either alter or paralyse these influences by introducing in the form of appropriate medicine the necessary ingredients which were likely to restore the patient to health.

It was held that the combinations and aspects of planets affect not only man, but also everything on the earth : animals, plants, stones, etc. . . . Thus, for example, a particular plant, or a stone was considered as a manifestation of a particular planetary influence.

All these influences were therefore classified as being of Mercurial, or Jupiterian, or Venusian, etc., nature. If by studying the horoscopic chart of a person, the sage saw that the affliction was caused by the weakening, for example, of the Jupiterian influence, owing to bad aspects at the precise moment of the sickness—he would try to restore the equilibrium by physical ingredients chosen among Jupiterian plants or salts, which had to be also in good correspondence with the nature of the subject. A small example may show that even in our days rational medicine employs the same ingredients as did the ancient science. But our doctor does not know *the reason* why certain ingredients exercise an effective power in a particular case. Contemporary medicine has found out by long observation and experiments the curative power of certain plants, whereas ancient science came to the same result by the study of the planetary influences which are manifested in the particular plants. Everyone knows the soothing effect of valerianum for all kinds of nervous affections. Well, the valerian plant is of the group of Mercury, and it is precisely this planet that affects the nervous centres of the human body. Thus in order to soothe an excitement, or great tension of nerves, the use of this particular plant (or of some other of the same planetary group) is indicated and was employed in ancient medicine.

It would take too long to go deeper into this question, and I refer those who are interested in the application of astrology to diagnosis and correct treatment to a very interesting book by a French doctor, M. Duz, *La Zodiologie Médicale*. This student of our contemporary purely rationalistic school consecrated long years to the study of astrology by means of which he could trace the different affections of the human body and establish a medicament, which is in correspondence with various diseases and also with the particular nature of the patient.

But all the different afflictions of the human being do not have their origin in the body, even those that apparently bear traces on the body, as, for example, erysipelas, a disease which seems to affect only the skin and which is very difficult to cure by ordinary means employed by our medicine. The apparent affection of the body is often only " a red flag," the sign of danger, showing that somewhere something has gone wrong. It would be folly and a disaster if a railway man, seeing the red flag, instead of trying to find out where is the danger, should simply concentrate his effort on destroying the sign of danger. Yet at the end of last century the doctors, noting a high temperature which the patient exhibited, started to give him quinine, or other chemicals which lower the fever. The high temperature is only the " red flag," showing that there is a process going on somewhere ; it is the reaction of vital forces which fight against the affection. Therefore, it is obvious that one must not paralyse this effort, but on the contrary, try and help the natural resistance. How many lives were lost owing to this essential error of treatment ? Happily, the doctors of the twentieth century understand this important point and the new school tries, not to stop the fever, but to trace the cause of it, and apply a remedy to the root of the trouble. But the source of the ailment resides very often not in the physical body, but in some other parts constituting man, though the body shows apparent signs of an affection. For this reason contemporary medicine is often incapable of curing some affections, as it rejects all idea of the complexity of the human being.

The convincing experiments of Colonel de Rochas, already mentioned in the previous chapter, showed the reality of the so-called "aura," or radiation of the human body. This aura constitutes a sort of envelope surrounding the body of man by a luminous nimbus. The colour of the aura in a sane man is, in general, reddish on the left side and bluish on the right, with a whole gamut of shades between, the different colouring being more or less distinct.

Observation of the aura pursued for a long time and on a great number of subjects showed the different coloration, especially in the region surrounding the head (its halo) which alters according to the state of health, or of momentary mental disturbance of the subject. This question was thoroughly studied and expounded in the works of de Rochas, Reichenbach, and others. According to the observations of these scientists the aura presents a constant current of what some call the "vital power" and others the "human magnetism." This power is exteriorised principally at the tips of fingers and toes, from which, as from the points of an electric machine, discharges in the form of sparks are ejected.

Those currents are very feebly luminous, but can be recorded by a special process on a photographic plate. Observations of these photographs show that in a normal state the currents form regular luminous lines along the hand and fingers which terminate at the tips of the fingers in little bunches of sparks. When man is not in a perfect state of health, or when he is disturbed by something (for example, by anger) the luminous lines get muddled up, presenting the aspect of uncombed hair. In certain affections which are difficult to treat by means of ordinary medicine, or cannot be treated at all—the observation of the aura shows the existence in it of dark spots corresponding to the affected part of the body. These spots indicate that the vital current is deranged in a certain place, and the effect of this disaccord is the visible disease on the physical body of the patient. Some call these spots in the aura " nests of astral microbes." It is natural that one must act upon the cause of the derangement in the aura and not upon the effect on the body which is only the " red flag." The effort of the orthodox medical man who tries to treat all forms of disease by applying physical remedies will naturally often be unsuccessful.

Some of the so-called " village medicine " is derived from knowledge inherited from the ancient wisdom. Though methods employed by these " witch doctors " might sometimes seem ridiculous—their effect is often quite wonderful. For example, in the case of erysipelas, the village sorcerer employed a red cloth, which he applied to the affected spot, then he traced on it with chalk the outlines of the inflamed spot and placed on the cloth something quickly inflammable (for example, some hemp in a very loose little heap). This heap was then burnt in a way not to injure the skin of the patient and, strange as it might seem, the erysipelas was cured. Though this might appear incredible, I can testify to having seen this process employed with complete success. The explanation of this curious method may be that the fire destroys the nest of astral microbes causing the disease, and thus the source of the affection being eliminated, the " red flag " on the body disappears of itself.

There exists in France a whole school which has put these proceedings on a scientific basis. After having observed the aura of the patient and located the nest of astral microbes, the doctor proceeds to burn them out by the means of a platinum plaque heated with electricity, which he moves over the affected place of the aura, not touching the body, that is to say, about half an inch from its surface.

To the treatment employed in cases of astral infections are related all so-called "sympathetic treatments." They consist in transporting a sickness from the man to an object or living being. These must be in perfect astrological correspondence with the affection and with the nature of the subject. Thus, for example, the jaundice, which is considered as a very severe disease necessitating a long treatment, can be cured in half an hour by transport of it on to a pike fish. I have had the opportunity of being present at one of these experiments. The patient was suffering from a very severe attack of jaundice, with high fever, and his face and the whites of the eyes were as yellow as lemon peel. A live pike was brought and placed before him in a basin containing water. He was seated before the basin and fixed his eyes upon the pike for some twenty or thirty minutes. Gradually his face became paler and paler, and during the same time the pike was turning as yellow as a lemon. At the end of the experiment the jaundice disappeared from the man and the pike was dead. You may smile at this strange statement, but I assure you that before having seen it done with my own eyes, I was as incredulous as you. Some very serious cases of hernia necessitating an operation were cured in ancient days by the transference of this malady to corresponding plants.

Different kinds of warts on the face and hands, which the ordinary doctor usually cuts or burns out, leaving scars on the skin, are taken away by sympathetic medicine and leave no trace at all on the affected spot.

I could multiply such examples as these which prove the effectiveness of sympathetic medicine, an effectiveness of which I have had many occasions to judge.

A medieval scholar, Paracelsus, wrote a whole book of different recipes of this kind, some of which are hard to understand, but some, which are comprehensible, prove to be wonderfully effective. For example, he composed a powder, which accelerates the healing of wounds and stops an infection of the blood. It can be employed with success in all kinds of abscesses, of bad wounds, and even in cases of damp eczema. For this purpose one took a bandage which had been applied to the wound, or abscess, and was soaked with the blood or matter of the patient. One treated it in a certain fashion with the mentioned powder, and the affection stopped very quickly and the wounded skin started healing three or four times as rapidly as it would have done with an ordinary treatment. This proceeding is called the treatment by " the mummy." The last is formed by the diseased matter taken from the body of the patient containing the noxious elements of the affection. One never applies the powder of Paracelsus to the affected part of the body, as this would injure the patient, but always to the liquid obtained from the injured spot. This treatment is of the order of " bewitchment," which I have expounded in the previous chapter, as every part of the body of man contains a particle of his personality. Thus in acting upon the infected blood by special agents, which destroy the infection—this curative action is transferred by sympathetic magic to the whole of the body, in which it kills the disease. To what a point the so-called " mummy " is attached to the man, from whom it has been taken, one can judge from the following modern experiment made with the powder of Paracelsus. The " mummy " of the patient was carried to a place far away from him (in the same town, but at a distance of about half an hour's walk), it was heated on the fire and immediately the patient felt an attack of fever and the thermometer showed a high temperature. Then one started to freeze the " mummy," putting it on ice, and the effect was identical, the patient complaining of being cold and starting to shiver. This experiment was carried out very carefully and scientifically under the direction of a doctor, and the different changes occurring to the patient in accordance with experiments made with the " mummy " were marked with precision. The exact time of these changes was checked by telephone connecting the two different places in which the operations were carried out.

Many treatments of the astral body, composing a whole branch of esoteric medicine, consist in the application of magnetic passes. Very many nervous affections can be cured by this method. The passes act as a kind of massage applied not to the physical body of the patient, but to his aura, or astral body. The magnetisers develop by constant practice their personal magnetism which constitutes one of the constructive forces active in every being. Thus by applying his hands over the patient in a certain way the magnetiser exteriorises his personal magnetism and reinforces the action of magnetic currents existing in the aura of the patient. The different ways of making these passes provoke either a soothing or an exciting effect on the sick person. This proceeding was well known and largely employed in ancient Egypt, and we can see on many frescoes the different gestures which the Egyptian doctors employed in different cases. The so-called " ka " position of extended hands is nothing else than the posture of a magnetiser acting on the backbone, or on the back of the head of the patient. On the well-known statue of Khephren in the Cairo Museum, we see the hawk, " Horus," enveloping the head of the Pharaoh with his wings extended in the posture of " ka." " The Ka of the god protects man from behind," says a text,

Fig. 28.

The *Ka* protecting the King Khephren. Cairo Museum.

and we read in the Gospels that Jesus felt " that virtue had gone out of Him " when He was touched in a crowd by a sick woman, who believed that she would be cured by the sole fact of touching the Saviour.

Thus the magnetic pass is a powerful means of treating all kinds of nervous affections. There exist in our days many schools where this kind of treatment is applied to subjects with success. The brothers Durville in Paris are renowned for their work on these lines.

I cannot dwell any longer on this subject of occult medicine and will now expound very shortly the last and most difficult part, the one that concerns the mental and spiritual part of man.

We know how powerless contemporary medicine is in the treatment of mental affections classified as different kinds of mania or insanity. There really does not exist any effective treatment for a case of madness. The doctors try all kinds of medicaments which have a more or less soothing effect upon the nervous system of the patient. But this effect can be only temporary and the treatment has only a palliative effect. In the lunatic asylums one puts the so-called mad people into a state in which they can do no harm by their eccentricity, and that is all. They are shut off from the normal activities of life under more or less decent conditions where they can vegetate.

To be able to treat a madman effectively, one must in the first place try to establish the cause of his insanity. This cause can arise from different sources, but in all cases it lies in a disharmony between the spiritual and the animal part of the being. To use a very rough comparison, man is composed of a series of envelopes, one contained within the other and more or less strongly bound together. According to the teaching of the Egyptians and also of the Cabala, man is composed of *nine* different envelopes. The most compact are those that are the lowest, of which the last is the physical body. The most etheric are the highest, and the most impalpable of them is the one that serves as the envelope or body to the reason of man. Between these two directly opposed poles there exists a whole scale of gradations, each of which exercises a particular function in the life of man : a double current circulates between the two opposed poles and animates the totality of the human being. One of these currents emanates from the reason of man and passing through his will realises his conception in the different acts executed by the body. The opposite current, born from the impressions received by the body through the different senses, carries these impressions to the reason, which makes from them the necessary deductions and sends orders to direct the corresponding action. In the animal, which presents a being composed of two parts : the soul and the physical body, but which is deprived of the Divine reason—in the animal, the reaction to the impressions received by the senses is carried out by the instinct, which is a part of the animic body.

Now imagine that the reason of man with its first envelope has for a moment left the body, which can happen either naturally during the sleep of man, or otherwise during experiments of the so-called " exteriorisation " of his etheric body. Then imagine that on coming back to its place of habitation, it finds this last occupied by some other either spiritual or elemental being. What will be the effect provoked by this occurrence ? Either the proprietor of the body chases out the intruder, or is chased out himself ; or otherwise both co-inhabit the body, sharing it between them. In the first case the subject, after a strange and incomprehensible disease, will suddenly become sane and normal again. In the second case he will become incurably insane and seem to have completely changed his individuality. In the third case he will be insane at certain moments, but sometimes will recover his normal state of lucidity. This will depend upon the struggle between the two inhabitants of the body, a fight in which either one or the other gains a temporary advantage.

In the Gospels we find an account of a man who was possessed, and out of whom Jesus chased " the legion of demons " and allowed them to go into a herd of swine. The different Christian churches, as well as those of antiquity, possess a special ritual in order " to cast out the devil " from a possessed person. I knew priests who had occasion to practise this terrifying ritual, and did so with success.

It is not necessarily the devil who enters into man, but it may be some sort of elemental being, of which there exists great numbers wandering about, and who are only seeking opportunities to get into possession of a material body in order to enjoy the lowest passions of physical life.

I have mentioned spiritism as operating in general with manifestations of different kinds of magnetic currents existing in man. In the rare cases of materialisations of beings of the other world during the spiritist séances, these are only low elementals, who try to enter into a momentary physical life, profiting by the vital current exteriorised by the medium. They call themselves by all sorts of names, they can take on different appearances, either of famous known men or of some relation of one of the sitters. These appearances are the creation of the thought of the living man who wants to see a particular being, but not the materialisation of the departed being itself.

The medieval magicians knew and employed various more or less complicated proceedings in order to materialise one of these elemental beings. The archives of the Inquisition are full of statements proving this dangerous practice, which was prevalent in monasteries and indulged in by monks and nuns who evoked the so-called " succubae and incubi," with which they entered into the most atrocious relations.

But let us come back to the cases of mania. The rituals employed by different churches in order to cast out the devil who took possession of man are all based on magic and *magic only*. Thus it is by means of this ancient science that one can cure certain cases of insanity. No treatment of any other kind, neither physical, by employing corresponding plants, nor any sympathetic or magnetic process, has any effect on this kind of case.

I cannot go deeper in this subject, but I want only to add one important observation. As we see from the Gospels, Christ allowed the devils which He chased out of man to enter into a herd of pigs—it is essential in every operation of this kind to prepare a physical abode into which the spirit or elemental cast out of man might enter. This abode need not necessarily be an animal. It can be a plant or even an object of some sort in correspondence with the nature of the subject. But one must provide some physical place of abode for the noxious being, otherwise the operator risks leaving it in a state in which it will continue to propagate its disastrous influence.

I hope that I have made it clear enough that the processes of ancient medicine, which are generally considered as foolish superstitions by our rational science, possess in reality a well-reasoned basis. Contemporary medicine recognises only a part of its ancient predecessor, the part that treats the physical body of man. It ignores all other possibilities of treatment than that of administering different chemical preparations more or less injurious to the living body. In this Homeopathy is on a more correct way than allopathy. In reducing medicaments and poisons to a state in which no chemical analysis can trace the presence of the medicament, *homeopathy acts by the soul and not by the body of the medicament.* Thus its action can attack some of the diseases which have their seat in the animic part of man. But certainly it is yet far from being able either to detect or to cure many affections.

Contemporary medicine can be compared to Astronomy. As the latter presents only the physical, or more correctly the mathematical part of ancient Astrology—our medicine is far from possessing all the different possibilities which were known and employed in the ancient curative art. This is due to the fact that, like all so-called rational sciences, contemporary medicine deals only with physical phenomena, ignoring totally all that concerns the higher parts of the complex composition of a human being.

CONCLUSION

AS the reader can judge, this little book cannot be considered as a treatise in which the ancient teaching is completely expounded. It only indicates the principal lines on which was based the wisdom of ancient schools of initiation.

Thus, to make comprehensible the symbolic expressions used in order to occult the tradition, I had to begin by outlining the principles on which was established the hieroglyphic writing of ancient Egypt. I began with the hieroglyphics, as it is the only writing in which we see the primitive ideographic image combined with a conventional grammatical sign into which in the course of time evolved all writing in general. The hieroglyphic writing is the only one known to us in which we can trace the gradual evolution of a tongue. That is the reason why I started this book by a sketch of this particular writing. But one must not think that this short outlook exhausts the vast subject which in our days presents a whole science called Egyptology.

My object was to show that our present knowledge of the Egyptian language is not sufficient; that the hieroglyphics possess far more than a grammatical meaning based upon their phonetic; that the point of view adopted by contemporary Egyptology enables us to read the texts and understand their phonetic meaning only, the one which was intended for the use of the uninitiated crowd. The symbolic meaning which contains the mysteries of ancient teaching cannot be understood if one employs only the method of orthodox Egyptology.

I am far from wishing to criticise these methods, and I recognise that they are indispensable in order to place on a solid foundation all possible research into such a difficult question as the comprehension of ancient symbolism. One must therefore start by studying the first meaning which we call " exoteric," but our study must not stop at this point. The one who wants to penetrate to the depths of the ancient thought has to carry on his research and first of all free himself from the idea that an ancient language, like the one used by the hierophants, was composed on the model of one of our contemporary, solely phonetic, languages. This preconceived idea, adopted by our learned men, led them into the error of under-valuing the ancient knowledge. The religious texts translated strictly and solely in their phonetic meaning present to us the teaching of Egyptian temples as being based upon a childish conception of the universe good enough for savages in a very low stage of mental evolution. This erroneous opinion cannot accord with the wonderful achievements of the Egyptians in architecture and mathematics in general, of which we can judge by the eternal monuments left by Egyptian civilisation. Then how can we explain the fact that all the Greek philosophers, who had received their initiation in Egypt, could develop their deep philosophic system which laid the foundation and oriented the thought of occidental humanity in the direction of abstract research for the hidden reasons of life. All the great thinkers of classic antiquity testify in concert that they had received the principles of their theories in the Egyptians' initiative schools. Surely they could not base their systems solely on some childish legends and myths which, to our idea, represent the religious teaching of the ancient temples. Evidently there must have been something else, something which is hidden from us, though it is constantly under our eyes, written on all the monuments and revealed in the way itself in which these last were built.

What would have been the sense in calling the hieroglyphic writing " the words of God " if it did not contain in itself revelations concerning the greatest secrets of creation?

Every one who starts the study of hieroglyphics is struck by the idea that our actual knowledge and method of their interpretation is insufficient, that these signs must contain much more than what is considered as being their meaning. The existing translation of all religious texts, beginning with those of the Pyramids, though made by conscientious and learned scholars, is quite unsatisfactory and cannot content anyone who wants to penetrate to the bottom of ancient thought. Even Champollion, the first to establish the principle of reading the phonetic meaning of hieroglyphics, even he felt that, apart from this first meaning, there existed other more occult meanings. He states this opinion in one of his first books, called *Précis du système hieroglyphique*, on pages 159–160.

But I repeat that the work of Champollion and of those who followed him was indispensable in order to establish the solid basis of understanding the grammatical composition of the tongue. Without this all efforts to penetrate into the symbolic meaning are apt to float in the air and risk becoming purely fantastic. We have many examples of this kind given, e.g. by the work of Kircher, an occultist of the seventeenth century, or of Ahmed Bin Aboubeker, an Arab scholar whose book was translated into English by J. Hammer and published in 1806. These two examples are sufficient to show how far a preconceived idea, unbased upon a solid foundation of knowledge, can lead to error and to purely fantastic deductions.

One cannot start ornamenting the walls of a house with frescoes before having built the walls themselves. Still less one can fill an unbuilt house with inhabitants. One can do it in imagination, but that kind of effort will be of the order of " castles in Spain."

Thus before starting to unravel the puzzles of the symbolic meaning, which presents the soul of the language, the student must study very thoroughly the exoteric or grammatical meaning of hieroglyphics given by Egyptology, the meaning which constitutes the skeleton, or the frame of the hieroglyphic writing.

The same concerns the Hebraic language, which I have outlined in the second part of the present book.

The generally adopted translation of the Bible based on the one of the " Septuagint " gives only the exoteric meaning of that wonderful book, meaning intended for the unprepared mind of the crowd. The peculiarity of the Hebraic alphabet, which I have tried to make evident, permitted of the combination in one word of several different meanings. Each of them could be understood by one who had received a special training, and a more or less philosophic orientation of the mind. The very renowned work of F. d'Olivet, which I have mentioned many times in the course of this book, enables us to understand how different combined meanings could coexist in a word. And his translation of the first ten chapters of Genesis serves as a luminous proof of the great value of that book, which presents itself in quite a new, purely scientific, and philosophic light.

The study of the principles of the Egyptian religion compared with those expressed in the Bible shows definitely that the latter was developed out of the former. But, as I have tried to show as clearly as possible, we cannot consider Egypt as being the cradle of religion or of science. Egypt is only one of the links in the universal chain of ancient tradition, the link that preceded the one constituted by the Hebraic Cabala. As I have shown, all the evidence which we find in the Egyptian texts and monuments seems to point to another yet anterior link of the same chain, and that link seems to be Atlantis.

This fabulous continent was situated somewhere in the Atlantic Ocean and from there, as from a centre, radiated its culture to the East as well as to the West. This would explain many difficult problems, and furnish the answer to the question why we find many common principles in the religions, arts, and sciences of different ancient civilisations separated one from another by enormous distances.

But we do not possess sufficient definite proofs to consider Atlantis as being the unique source and cradle of primitive teaching. It seems more reasonable to suppose that this civilisation was again only a branch from the mother root, and that another branch was in Lemuria.

As Atlantis spread its civilisation on the continents of America, Europe, and round the borders of the Mediterranean, Lemuria was the centre from which originated the Oriental civilisations of Asia. But some points that we can trace in the Occidental branch, and which are common to the Oriental branch, seem to prove that at the origin of prehistory there existed on earth one unique civilisation based probably on the primitive revelation and which in far-off prehistoric times divided itself in the Atlantean and Lemurian cultures.

This seems to be obvious if we observe the principles of art common to all known civilisations on earth, and also those of writing and phonetic which we can trace in languages, which to our knowledge had developed in their own particular way, not being derived one from another.

The object of my present book is to establish the point of view that all our knowledge expressed either in art, or in science, or in religious principles, is an inheritance which we have received from one source, the primitive revelation. To be able to understand this point of view and to trace this last through the scattered links of the lost chain of ancient tradition, it is necessary to study the ancient languages, the ancient art, and the religious doctrines of the different teaching of antiquity.

The reader remembers from what I have said already that the ancient priest was simultaneously a scholar and that all science was born in temples and presented the appanage of the priest.

Thus the general plan of this book becomes clear and logical. We have begun by a rapid review of the principles that constituted two distinct writings, one developed out of the other, but each presenting its own particularity. Then we passed over the principles of religious teaching and philosophy of the same two civilisations. And at last we saw how these ideas were adapted for the realisation of the principle in the form of art and different so-called " occult sciences."

I repeat that this little book does not pretend to exhaust the vast subject which it outlines. It gives only a schematic general idea and each chapter can be developed in a big separate work.

Those who would want to continue their study in one particular branch of knowledge indicated in the chapters of the present book will have to address themselves to other more complete works. Concerning the symbolic meaning of hieroglyphics, they will find more detailed notions in my works published in French, but which will probably soon appear in English. I allow myself to recommend these books only because outside my work there does not yet exist any book which treats the same subject of the symbolic meaning of hieroglyphics based on the roots of contemporary Egyptology and not in contradiction with the discoveries of that science.

Concerning the Hebraic teaching and essentially the Cabala, there exists a great number of books written in different languages, both in medieval times and in our days. The best book treating this subject, to my knowledge, is the one I have mentioned already many times and which came from the pen of F. d'Olivet. I recommend everyone who is interested in the study of the Hebraic writing and who wants to penetrate the mysteries of the Cabala as well as of the different occult sciences, to take as a starting-point the work of this eminent writer. After having studied it one can be sure that one has placed oneself on a solid and true basis and that in developing the principles established by this work one does not risk falling into a pit of error in the very difficult research to be undertaken in the domain of occult science based on the Hebraic tradition.

The third part of the present book is the logical development of the first two parts, giving general ideas concerning some sciences which constituted the ancient teaching and which were represented by means of symbolic writing. I have tried to show that the different applications of the sacred and secret knowledge constituted in old days the highest scientific accomplishment and therefore were reserved to the possession of priests. In old days the one who wanted to study one of these sacred sciences had to prove that he was worthy of receiving instruction in the superior wisdom and that in no case he would employ it for low and harmful objects. The novice had to pass through many different tests in the schools of initiation, and only after these tests were entrusted to him little by little, the great secrets of nature were revealed and the knowledge of how to use the corresponding supernatural powers. This initiation naturally took a long time. We possess a document written by Baken-Khonsou, a high priest of the Theban temple, who gives some details concerning his career. He entered the service of the temple, being sixteen years old, as novice (*ouab*), and was for four years in that preparatory stage. At the age of twenty he attained the first grade of priesthood and remained in it for twelve years. At thirty-two he became the third prophet of Amon, which office he exercised for fifteen years. At forty-seven he was elevated to the rank of second prophet of Amon and carried out this duty for twelve years. At last at fifty-nine he attained the high degree of first prophet of Amon, which office he held for twenty-seven years, till the end of his days. He considered himself very lucky in having climbed the ladder of initiation in such a short time. How many were there that could only attain one of the first degress and stayed in it for the rest of their lives ?

From this statement you can judge for yourself with what difficulty could be obtained the initiation even in the old days when there existed initiative schools and when the student received individual training according to his particular capacities.

Nowadays, when there no longer exist any initiative schools, when the student has to study under the conditions of our complicated materialistic life, it is natural that his work is still harder; he must base his studies upon what he finds written on the subject that interests him, and he has only his sense of intuition to guide him on the way. He has got to eliminate by his own judgment what he considers as being erroneous and choose only what seems to lead him to the knowledge of Truth. A student is lucky if he finds a master who has already attained a certain elevation on the ladder of knowledge and who will direct him in his research. But how many of these so-called " masters " are only charlatans, or even worse—false prophets, whose purpose is to lead the novice into erroneous ways tending to disaster. Thus one must be very careful in the choice of initiatory books and of a putative master if one wants to avoid a false step and a fall into a pit, instead of attaining the enlightenment that one is seeking for.

The knowledge is possible of attainment, but the way to it requires a constant effort and a clear judgment on the part of one who seeks the true illumination. Even the best intentions may produce the opposite result to the one desired, if the seeker chooses the wrong path.

This is a friendly warning from one who has consecrated all his life to the study of these questions, and who has read more or less all the serious works that have been written in different languages concerning the occult sciences.

THE END

CPSIA information can be obtained
at www.ICGtesting.com
Printed in the USA
BVHW070247220620
581990BV00002B/99

9 781162 583686